The Distilleries of Vancouver Island

THE
DISTILLERIES
OF VANCOUVER
ISLAND

A Guided Tour of West Coast Craft and Artisan Spirits

Marianne Scott

x

TOUCHWOOD

TouchWood Editions
touchwoodeditions.com

The information in this book is true and complete to the best of the
author's knowledge. All recommendations are made without
guarantee on the part of the author or the publisher.

Edited by Meg Yamamoto
Interior design by Sydney Barnes
Except where otherwise indicated, photos appear courtesy of the author.

CATALOGUING INFORMATION AVAILABLE FROM
LIBRARY AND ARCHIVES CANADA

ISBN 9781771513326 (softcover)
ISBN 9781771513357 (electronic)

TouchWood Editions acknowledges that the land on which we live and
work is within the traditional territories of the Lkwungen (Esquimalt
and Songhees), Malahat, Pacheedaht, Scia'new, T'Sou-ke and WSÁNEĆ
(Pauquachin, Tsartlip, Tsawout, Tseycum) peoples.

We acknowledge the financial support of the Government of Canada through
the Canada Book Fund and of the Province of British Columbia through the
Book Publishing Tax Credit.

Printed in China

This book was produced using FSC®-certified, acid-free papers, processed
chlorine free, and printed with soya-based inks.

25 24 23 22 21   1 2 3 4 5

To all the Vancouver Island and Gulf Islands
spirit entrepreneurs who generously
shared their time and tipples

NANAIMO REGION

WEST COAST VANCOUVER ISLAND

TOWARD CAMPBELL RIVER

CAMPBELL
RIVER 21

COURTENAY 20

19

HORNBY ISLAND

TOFINO
17

16

15

PARKSVILLE

UCLUELET 18

NANAIMO 14

SALT
SPRING
ISLAND

11 10

9 13

DUNCAN

12

8

7

COBBLE
HILL

6

1

VICTORIA

SOOKE

5

4

2 3

1   Sheringham Distillery, *Sooke*
2   Macaloney's Caledonian Distillery & Twa Dogs
     Brewery, *Victoria*
3   Moon Distillery, *Victoria*
4   Phillips Fermentorium Distilling Company, *Victoria*
5   Spinnakers, *Victoria*
6   DEVINE Distillery & Winery, *Saanichton*
7   Victoria Distillers, *Sidney*
8   Merridale Cidery & Distillery, *Cobble Hill*
9   Goldstream Distillery, *Duncan*
10   Stillhead Distillery, *Duncan*
11   Ampersand Distilling Company, *Duncan*
12   Salt Spring Shine Craft Distillery, *Salt Spring Island*
13   Sweetwater Distillery, *Salt Spring Island*
14   Arbutus Distillery, *Nanaimo*
15   Bespoke Spirits House, *Parksville*
16   Misguided Spirits Craft Distillery, *Parksville*
17   Tofino Distillery, *Tofino*
18   Pacific Rim Distilling, *Ucluelet*
19   Island Spirits Distillery, *Hornby Island*
20   Wayward Distillery, *Courtenay*
21   Shelter Point Distillery, *Campbell River*

INTRODUCTION

IT WAS IN 2016 THAT I FIRST BECAME aware of the craft and artisan distilleries proliferating on Vancouver Island, where I live. I visited Victoria Distillers, whose stills had just moved to the Sidney waterfront. The spacious tasting room with its large expanse of windows offers an enthralling view of the Gulf and San Juan Islands with a snow-covered Mount Baker towering in the distance. The copper-and-stainless-steel stills surge toward the ceiling. The master distillers offer tours and tell spirit lovers how the company makes its vodka, gins, oaken gin, and chocolate liqueur, among other elixirs. It was my introduction to the process of distilling—the multiple steps it requires and the art and science behind it.

During the tour, Master Distiller Leon Webb held a cup under the spout of one of the stills. We sniffed the clear liquid with its potent scent—it was way too strong to drink. "It's the last bit of gin we've just distilled," Webb told us. "The distilled product is made up of heads, hearts, and tails. Only the heart, the middle of the distilled liquid, is drinkable. You'll sample some form of that in the tasting room." (In Great Britain, the heads are often called foreshots, and the tails, feints.)

At Victoria Distillers, though, all three parts of the distillate are used. The first part, the heads, contains toxic methanol and is recycled as biofuel; the last part, the tails, is redistilled in the next batch. Other distillers have different methods of reusing or disposing of the distillate's undrinkable components.

A year later, I went on the road and visited the nine other craft and artisan distilleries on Vancouver Island, describing their operations and products in an article for *British Columbia Magazine*. I learned much more about the distilling process, how the producers decided to become spirit entrepreneurs, what they selected as their base ingredients, and how they strive to make their liquors unique. I was charmed by the ardour these entrepreneurs bring to their spirited craft. I acquired a taste for the yeasty, heady scents of fermenting grains, wine, fruit, and honey.

Since my voyage to those 10 Vancouver Island craft and artisan producers, 11 more distilleries have launched or are launching their enterprises in the region—now including the Gulf Islands—all attempting to engender their own spirits with authenticity and character. More distilleries may be in the planning stage. These entrepreneurs are capitalizing on the movement toward enjoying locally and regionally produced food and drink.

Mass-produced foodstuffs don't offer the same freshness and innovative taste often found in handmade artisan fare. It's one of the reasons craft brewers and craft distillers have developed a following: their beverages aren't concocted in colossal, computer-controlled megafactories, which tend to produce uniform, standardized-tasting liquor. Experimentation with different ingredients and flavourings to fashion distinct tipples can be achieved only in small-batch distilleries using the distiller's ingenuity.

HOW I APPROACHED THIS BOOK

In *The Distilleries of Vancouver Island*, I tell you a lot about the distillers themselves, along with their products. I describe how they became interested in their craft, their formal or informal educational background in spirit making, their views on what makes their techniques and products unique, their dedication to sustainability, their family support and involvement, and their business plans and coworkers.

The British Columbia craft and artisan distillery industry is young. The two oldest small-batch distilleries, Merridale Cidery & Distillery and Victoria Distillers, obtained their licences in 2007. Specific *craft* distilling licences became available only in 2013, when BC updated parts of its liquor laws. Thus the distillers are taking a risk in a new industry, one that doesn't offer many blueprints for success, and that requires significant investment.

Yet these craft and artisan distillers have taken the gamble, even with few role models to emulate. They are creating jobs for themselves. They support the local economy by generating employment and paying taxes. They encourage agri-tourism. They are devoted to the sustainability of locally grown ingredients, with short delivery routes. I hope their stories will inspire others to become spirit entrepreneurs and serve as role models.

HOW ALCOHOL DISTILLATION WORKS

The process for producing ethanol—the distillation process—separates alcohol from water using evaporation and condensation. Ethanol, also known as ethyl alcohol, grain alcohol, pure alcohol, or neutral spirits, is the basic liquid needed to make all high-alcohol-content beverages—it's the stuff that ends up in all liquors and liqueurs made in the world. To produce ethanol is a step-by-step process that demands all the art and science a distiller can marshal.

THE BASE

A distiller must first choose ingredients that form the base of the eventual ethanol. Many grains, fruits, and vegetables can serve as base, including barley, wheat, buckwheat, corn, rye, grapes, wine, cider, honey, potatoes, sugar cane, sugar beets, sorghum, the agave plant, maple syrup, and even rice. The choice of base is often directly connected to its locale: tequila, for example, is distilled from the juice of the agave plant, which grows in several Mexican states. Quebec has spawned a maple syrup liqueur. Liquor becomes a liqueur—like Baileys, Grand Marnier, Drambuie, and Frangelico—when bottled with added sugars of some kind and flavourings. In some localities, fruits such as apples, plums, and peaches also serve as raw material; many eaux-de-vie or schnapps derive from these fruits.

MALTING

Barley is one of the most commonly used grains for malting. To make malt, the barley is first sprouted with water and then dried. The grain is usually milled, or crushed, to increase its surface area. This grist is added to hot water in a mash tun, where the grains' enzymes convert their starch to fermentable sugars. The tun has external heating and cooling mechanisms that help saccharification (turning starch to sugar). The tun also contains an agitator—think old-fashioned washing machine—to mix the ingredients and ensure they are uniformly wetted. The liquid that's drained off is called the wort.

The next step places the wort into a fermenting tank, where yeast and/or enzymes are added. The length of the fermentation process depends on what's in the wort but usually lasts from three to seven days (distillers using honey as their base ferment for up to three weeks). The leftover liquid—water and alcohol—called the wash, is then pumped into a still. By volume, the wash contains roughly 6–20 percent alcohol; the rest is water.

DISTILLING

Once in the still, the wash is heated. Ethanol boils at 78.4°C (173.1°F), while water boils at 100°C (212°F). The difference in the boiling points separates the ethanol from the water and makes the alcohol concentration in the vapour phase higher than the water content. Often, the distiller does a stripping run, which removes a portion of the wash's water. The result of this first run is called the low wine.

THE STILLS

Two main types of stills distill the wash: the pot still and the column still. They have the same function: to create a difference in boiling points that allows them to separate ethanol from water.

The pot still is the most traditional—its various forms and shapes have been used for centuries—and is usually made of copper. It produces a single batch of ethanol. The pot still has a main chamber—the pot—where the wash is heated by an internal coil until the alcohol separates from the water as a vapour; the vapour rises to the top of the still. From there, the vapour runs through a pipe—the lyne arm. A cooling coil returns the vapour to its liquid state—the distillate—which in turn is collected in a vessel ready for further processing. Many distillates are distilled a second or third time to reach 90 percent purity or higher. Certain spirits, including Scotch malt whiskies, Irish whiskey, and cognac, *must* be distilled in a copper pot still. That said, I have seen several stills that have been adapted to be both pot stills and column stills. Some stainless steel pots pack copper coils in the column to give the distillate copper exposure. Others have a removable stainless steel column that can be replaced with a copper head.

The column still, invented in the early 1800s, is vertical and often much taller than a pot still. It's usually fabricated from stainless steel, or in combination with copper. A column still typically contains a series of chambers, plates, or coils and has a reflux condenser positioned at its top. Each time the vapour percolates through the column, it recondenses, thereby intensifying the spirit's purity and potency. It can condense the alcohol to the desired strength—from 90 percent up.

When the distillate leaves the still, the producer sniffs and tastes the product to avoid mixing heads or tails with the hearts. This is a careful process requiring great skill. In past times, when homemade stills brewed up moonshine and when "bathtub gin" became popular during US Prohibition, poisoning from the distillate's methanol-containing heads was not uncommon.

The ethanol hearts leaving a column still can be bottled as vodka, transformed into gin by spicing it with juniper and other botanicals, made into brandy and liqueurs, or modified by additions such as coffee, almonds, fruit, chocolate, or other flavourings. Blending different batches of alcohol is another common method of changing the flavour of a beverage.

The ethanol hearts leaving a pot still are mostly used for whisky. To be legally certified as whisky, the ethanol leaving the still must mature at least three years in a wooden barrel.

Many whiskies are aged well beyond three years—usually increasing their desirability and cost. Some whiskies are matured quickly, and the "new makes" do win prizes. The casks storing the whisky can be made of various woods, usually oak, may use raw wood or a charred interior, and may previously have contained such beverages as bourbon, sherry, rum, port, or wine. The type of wood and the barrels' previous uses will affect the colour, flavour, aroma, and smoothness of the final product.

THE HISTORY OF DISTILLING

Alcohol distilling has a long history, although its earliest beginnings are murky. Hard liquor does not appear in the Bible, although wine is mentioned as early as the fifth chapter of Genesis. The parable of Jesus changing water into wine suggests that wine has had differing levels of quality for millennia. Chemical analysis of a 9,000-year-old pot found in China showed it once held an alcohol-containing drink. Our Neolithic ancestors knew how to ferment sugar into alcohol. The difference between their concoctions and today's products is that our ancient ancestors didn't distill beverages whose alcohol-by-volume content rose much higher than 16 percent. Today, the most potent liquors may contain 96–98 percent alcohol by volume (that's up to 196 proof), although the average bottle of hooch we buy at the farm gate or liquor store ranges from 37 to 50 percent alcohol by volume.

Distilling other materials also took place over thousands of years—the Romans distilled pine oil to make turpentine. Distillation has been used to desalinate water, formulate perfumes, and increase the alcohol content of wine. The discovery of a 12th-century still in China proves distillation was known in

Asia, while India imported its distillation craft from the Middle East; it had spread widely by the 14th century.

Alchemists practising during the Middle Ages searched for methods that would transmute lesser metals into gold. Although they were unsuccessful, their use of distillation and continual experimentation eventually led to the science of chemistry.

According to the December 18, 2003, edition of the *Economist*, Arabic science is responsible for developing and disseminating the art of alcohol distilling: "It may be that the single most pervasive legacy of Islamic civilisation is not holy scripture, but the rather unholy art of distilling alcohol. Not only were Arabs the first to make spirits. The great trading civilisation of Islam spread the skill across the globe." (The term *alcohol* is derived from Arabic, as is *alchemist*.)

By 1200, spirit distillation was well known and the science proliferated across Europe. Wikipedia reports that "in 1500, German alchemist Hieronymus Braunschweig published *Liber de arte destillandi* (*The Book of the Art of Distillation*), the first book solely dedicated to the subject of distillation."

Although it's generally believed that alcohol was brought to the Americas by Europeans, the Indigenous population had developed various alcoholic drinks, made from corn and honey, but of fairly low alcohol content. The European conquerors imported "firewater" with its potent alcohol levels.

Today, massive multibillion-dollar factories producing millions of litres of spirits dominate the world market. As in many industries, mergers and acquisitions have consolidated liquor brands under one roof. Some of these giant companies are little known in the West; for example, China's Kweichow Moutai focuses its sales of the popular sorghum-and-wheat-based spirit Moutai on local markets. From its Paris headquarters,

Pernod Ricard manages globally produced brands like Beefeater, Absolut, Jameson, Havana Club, and Chivas Regal. The largest of all, London-based Diageo, annually sells 6.5 billion litres of spirits from more than 100 sites in 30 countries, marketing such brands as Johnnie Walker, Crown Royal, J&B, Smirnoff, Ketel One, and Captain Morgan.

THE CONUNDRUM OF APPLYING FOR SPIRIT AWARDS

To add prestige and increase sales, some of the regional craft distilleries send in samples of their spirits to the many competitions held around the world. It may pay off spectacularly, as it did for Sheringham Distillery, whose Seaside Gin was named the World's Best Contemporary Gin at the 2019 World Gin Awards in London. Sheringham's gin has seen huge sales growth. But for some distillers still early in their growth phase, the award game is a gamble—it's a costly and time-consuming process.

I checked a few contests to determine the cost of entry fees. A single entry into the 2020 San Francisco World Spirits Competition, for example, is US$550. To enter the International Wine & Spirit Competition in London, the fee including value-added tax is about $275. The London Spirits Competition runs about $300 per entry. Fees for entries into more regional contests are generally lower, but these events do not carry the prestige of the big international competitions. Then there are packaging and freight costs, international customs permits, fees and duty, and many forms to complete. It's tough for a new craft distillery, but it may be worth the effort.

BRITISH COLUMBIA'S LIQUOR LAWS

In 2013, British Columbia changed its liquor laws and licences, and for the first time, craft distilling became a legally permitted and financially worthwhile enterprise. The new licensing has created a boom in craft distilleries, with more opening every year.

Two categories of distilleries—commercial and craft—are the designated entities. The commercial distilleries have no limit on production and can source their fermentation ingredients from anywhere they wish. But many of these remain "artisan," in that they continue to make small-batch spirits on-site, with their own specific flavourings. All distilleries may sell direct to consumers from their on-site store.

A craft distillery, however, receives tax benefits for its first 50,000 litres of spirits produced each year. In addition, craft distilleries are required to use 100 percent BC agricultural products to make their alcohol. Flavourings may come from outside the province. All products made by the distillery must be fermented and distilled at the licensed distillery site. All products must be produced using traditional distilling techniques; neutral grain spirits must be distilled on-site. (Neutral grain spirits are bulk alcohol produced and sold by industrial distilleries; they allow some distillers to bypass the craft of producing fermentable mash to create their own alcohol.) These regulations are designed to support British Columbia's wide-ranging agriculture, tourism, and small businesses.

The rules also stipulate that any business making spirits must obtain a distillery licence from the Liquor and Cannabis Regulation Branch. In addition, the distillery must qualify for a federal excise tax licence and tax number.

Distilleries of any size may set up a tasting room where samples are offered to visitors. Sample tasting cannot exceed 15 millilitres of spirits, with a maximum of 45 millilitres per person per day. The reporting requirements for all aspects of spirit making and selling are extensive.

Distilleries can also give tours of their premises and explain their unique libations to patrons while offering samples. They can apply for an on-site retail store permit as well. Some distillers have opted to include a cocktail lounge on their premises, which requires an additional licence.

A few microdistillers sell their alcohol through the BC Liquor Distribution Branch, but others say they cannot afford the fees charged—up to 160 percent—and still run a viable business. Instead they sell their products on-site, to private liquor stores and restaurants, and at farmers' markets, where profitability is higher.

HOW TO USE THIS BOOK

On the map, you can see the distribution of craft and artisan distilleries across Vancouver Island and the Gulf Islands. They are arranged by region, allowing visitors to group one or more distilleries per day. If you live in a certain area of Vancouver Island, you can make day trips to nearby distilleries or make them part of a longer voyage. If you arrive on Vancouver Island by ferry, boat, or plane, you can plan routes that allow spirit tours over several days. One caution: always check the websites to determine if the distilleries are open. Some have restricted hours.

The Victoria area's distilleries are located within a few kilometres of each other, and you might visit more than one a day. Moon Distillery, Phillips Fermentorium, and Spinnakers are in downtown Victoria, while Macaloney's Caledonian Distillery is located in Saanich, a few kilometres north of downtown Victoria. For a splendid day on the Saanich Peninsula, consider a tour and tastings at DEVINE Distillery & Winery in Saanichton and Victoria Distillers in Sidney.

Starting from Victoria, I recommend a day trip out to Sheringham Distillery in Sooke, where you can also explore such places as Sooke Potholes Provincial Park and East Sooke Regional Park. Or you can incorporate a visit to Sooke, the Cowichan Valley, and Duncan while travelling the Pacific Marine Circle Route. A Vancouver Island trip north (from Victoria) and then west to the Pacific Rim National Park Reserve's beaches may include a stop at Misguided Spirits Craft Distillery on Route 4A and then the Tofino and Ucluelet distilleries. In the Nanaimo region, you can start with Arbutus Distillery in Nanaimo, then drive north to Bespoke Spirits House in Parksville, Wayward Distillery in Courtenay, and Shelter Point Distillery in Campbell River, with a side trip to Island Spirits Distillery on Hornby Island. Alternatively, travelling south from Nanaimo, you'll find Ampersand Distilling, Stillhead Distillery, Goldstream Distillery, and Merridale Cidery & Distillery located fairly close to one another. A visit to Salt Spring Island's famous farmers' market can incorporate side trips to Salt Spring Shine Craft Distillery and Sweetwater Distillery. Undoubtedly, you'll use your imagination to organize other voyages that combine artisan food and wine with craft spirits.

I have avoided describing the taste of the many spirits created by our craft and artisan distilleries. Taste, after all, is highly personal. What may be my favourite gin tastes like gasoline to others. Moreover, I find the language touting the benefits of alcoholic drinks is often over the top, too florid, too baroque. Thus I'm leaving taste descriptions to your personal ingenuity. Many distilleries' websites offer tasting notes.

TOO MUCH OF A GOOD THING

Visiting a distillery, or multiple distilleries, can be an intoxicating adventure. Literally. So when you use this book to guide you on a distillery tour, carefully select your venues and the distances between them. Once there, drink only enough to taste the spirit, a tiny sip—enough to wet your tongue—then discard any liquid left in your glass. Remember that in British Columbia, you must be 19 years of age to drink alcohol.

Make sure you have a designated driver who doesn't imbibe. I found two distilleries a day to be the maximum, with a solid breakfast, and an ample lunch between a morning and an afternoon visit. Make your distillery visits a delight, not a funeral.

As the American journalist and novelist Jonathan Miles said, "For me, alcohol has this endless fascination that there's this substance that can enhance life so beautifully and destroy it so completely."

VICTORIA REGION

1
SHERINGHAM DISTILLERY

JASON AND ALAYNE MACISAAC
OWNERS AND DISTILLERS

252–6731 WEST COAST ROAD

SOOKE, BC V9Z 0S9

778-425-2019

SPIRITS@SHERINGHAMDISTILLERY.COM

SHERINGHAMDISTILLERY.COM

LATITUDE 48.375532, LONGITUDE -123.724214

JASON MACISAAC, WHEN SERVING AS CHEF AT THE
Point-No-Point restaurant in Shirley, BC, found a few abandoned
jugs. He'd unearthed them from a dilapidated shack on the
property of the house he rented in Jordan River. The jugs were the
old gallon-sized glass ones, with a handle to thread your finger
through. Intrigued, he wondered if they were evidence of past
moonshining.

Jason asked Point-No-Point's owner if illicit alcohol production had been popular in this isolated stretch of Vancouver
Island edging Juan de Fuca Strait. He learned a flock of stills was
once active in the region. There was even a still in the basement of the old Jordan River Hotel, and its hard liquor was sold
upstairs in the bar, making it a popular watering hole before it
burned down in 1984.

Later, as explained on Sheringham's website, Jason discovered that the cabin he'd rented was built in the late 1930s
and that the original
owners of the cabin
operated a gold-col-
lecting sluice box at a
nearby creek. If they'd
had a successful year
amassing gold tidbits,
they'd buy whisky for
the local community's
New Year's Eve cel-
ebration. Thus, in
reverse alchemy, gold
turned into whisky.

Jason and Alayne MacIsaac.
Photo: Gilda Good.

Jason was inspired by the rum-running lore during US Prohibition in this sparsely populated part of the coast and the tales of stills producing moonshine in the woods or hidden sheds. He felt a burning curiosity about the distilling process and decided he *had* to build a still. He ordered a manual on still construction and distillate collection from a chemist in New Zealand, where home distilling is legal.

THE FIRST STILL

In the early 2000s, with a bundle of copper pipes from Home Hardware and a water-heater boiler, Jason assembled his still. He describes it as an off-the-shelf project, copper with silver solder, certainly not beautiful, but functional. His maiden booze run worked. "At least after the first batch," he quips. Building the homemade still and creating his homemade firewater served as his distillery apprenticeship.

He recalled his homemade libation being a decent product and imbibed it only at home and with friends. He never sold his hooch, but he did obtain a distilled-spirits permit with a dream of opening a distillery one day. Meanwhile, he substituted his career as restaurant executive chef with his own catering business, serving as a private chef for family, corporate, and elite parties.

In 2008, Jason and Alayne began dating, while she continued to run her Vancouver wholesale clothing company, marketing her wares throughout BC and Alberta. After the couple married in 2011, Alayne began thinking about new opportunities on Vancouver Island, seriously considering a food-related business. Their daughter, Cassandra, was born in 2013, and being parents became part of the couple's life.

LAUNCHING THE DISTILLERY

During one of his private-chef events, Jason learned that new BC laws were allowing individuals to establish craft distilleries. After intense discussions with Alayne, and careful consideration of their finances, Jason applied for a licence. Working with the Capital Regional District (CRD) in Sooke was a challenge, as existing laws on alcohol production had been created for large distillers, not farm-gate producers.

Zoning issues like big-truck traffic, smokestacks, and impacts on residential neighbourhoods were raised. "These just didn't apply to us," says Jason. "There was no real model. We were breaking ground. The CRD and we had to learn together how the new zoning and regulations applied to microproducers in our district, to reconcile what *we* wanted with what *they* wanted."

Fortunately, the CRD was supportive and after about 18 months issued the necessary licences to produce, sell, and store spirits. In 2015, Jason and Alayne opened their distillery.

I first met the MacIsaacs in 2017, when they operated their still in the coach house next to their dwelling in Shirley overlooking Juan de Fuca Strait. They named their company after the original name for their hamlet, Sheringham. It was renamed Shirley when the previous moniker was too long to fit on a postage stamp. The nearby Sheringham Point Lighthouse, built in 1912 and still warning ships away from the rocks, carries the earlier name.

It was the couple's proximity to salt water that inspired their theme, "coastal craft spirits." As their base, they use 80 percent raw wheat and 20 percent malted (sprouted) barley, which at the time of my 2017 visit was supplied by Gambrinus Malting in Armstrong, BC. Everything was done by hand, from loading the grains, yeast, and hot water into the mash tuns, to stirring the mash with a rowboat paddle, to transferring the fermented product (called "wash") into the still for the distillation process. Spent grain was recycled as cattle feed at regional farms.

As the clear spirit dribbles out a stainless steel spout, Jason judges when the "heads" (the mostly methanol liquid that first emerges from the still) turns into the "heart," the good, usable ethanol, and then into "tails," the lower-alcohol portion, which may also include unpleasant odours. "The art of distillation is deciding where to make the 'cut' between heads, hearts, and tails," says Jason. "My chef's palate helps me decide when." He depends on his culinary background, founded in French traditional food, skills, and recipes, as a foundation for becoming an expert judge of the distillate's three stages.

MOVING TO SOOKE

After just three years in the Shirley facility, having won several prizes for its gin and akvavit, the distillery had outgrown the coach house and moved its operation to Sooke. It's the westernmost distillery in Canada. Sheringham now occupies a former automotive repair shop. The car hoists were removed, and the walls and ceilings painted a bright white. Revised and upgraded plumbing was installed, and an office was tucked into a corner.

Sheringham's tasting room.

The new premises appear modest from the outside, but the tasting room is cheerful and inviting. Shelves behind the bar display the distillery's products, including an array of clear bottles showing the botanicals that flavour its gins. The MacIsaacs are pleased with the new workspace; they can ramp up as the company expands.

The distilling room is home to three stills: a copper pot still used for the stripping (first) run, a column still for second distillations, an aromatic still for gin and Lumette (more about that later), and a variety of stainless steel mash and fermenting tanks. The stills are fabricated by Wenzhou Yayi, a light-industrial manufacturer located in Wenzhou, China, a city with more than nine million inhabitants. "Some of my BC colleagues recommended this firm," says Jason. "The stills have been great, and so has the service and backup."

Mounds of white bags secured from South Peace Grain, containing specially designed distilling wheat and ordered by the tonne, are stacked on their pallets. Malted barley, prepared at Phillips Brewing & Malting in Victoria, is delivered every two weeks. Phillips's barley is grown mostly on the Saanich Peninsula and thus also meets the "made-in-BC" requirement for locally grown grains.

The bottling station flanks the stills, and hand-tied cards, each offering an enticing cocktail recipe, festoon all the bottles. The band covering the cork displays an image of the schooner *Favorite*, built in 1886 in Victoria. A large cistern allows the distillery to recirculate water from the stills.

Jason runs the spirit-production side while Alayne, with her long experience in marketing and sales, manages the business aspects. She developed the distillery's solid business plan and arranges the day-to-day logistics. To make sure all the distilling ingredients are on hand, Jason orders the grains, botanicals, and other elements necessary to make their spirits. Alayne, meanwhile, supervises the staff who fill and label the bottles, among other tasks. She manages the finances, distribution of their products, marketing to private liquor stores, and staffing of their booths at five farmers' markets.

Sheringham's distilling equipment.

The MacIsaacs live in an apartment above the distillery. It's convenient because the stills, when operating, need strict supervision for safety as well as quality. The stills are never left unattended.

Sheringham's new Sooke location is more easily accessible to people wishing to tour the distillery and purchase their spirits on-site. The couple wants to further stimulate tourism in the Sooke region; the distillery is an easy stop for tourists travelling the south Vancouver Island Pacific Marine Circle Route.

THE CHALLENGES OF STARTING A DISTILLERY

The MacIsaacs aren't shy about discussing the challenges of starting a craft distillery. "Many people think that making spirits is sexy and very lucrative," says Alayne. "We are doing well and pay our staff well. But during the summer when hordes of tourists stop by for a taste and a tour, we work seven days a week. And we're not becoming millionaires."

Jason adds he and Alayne are equally devoted to the business, but that means there is equal stress. Managing growth, finding storage space, scheduling the deliveries, taste-testing the distillates—there's no relief, and that can lead to being tired and tapped out. "We've had to learn to communicate better as a couple," he says. "We're like the old-fashioned family business but need to guard against being totally absorbed by that business, take time to regroup."

The couple has recommendations for others wishing to launch a distillery. Although it's a cliché, they say, doing your homework is key. Develop a sound business plan. Talk to other distillers (but make an appointment first). Assess your finances and how long you can operate before making a profit. Ask where you want to be in five years.

SHERINGHAM'S STANDARD PRODUCTS

Sheringham's vodka—the first liquid that comes out of the still—is highly purified and contains hints of citrus and vanilla. Alcohol by volume is 40 percent.

Sheringham's products.

The uniquely flavoured Seaside Gin is Sheringham's flagship product. To create this elixir, Jason begins with the purified ethanol and infuses the botanicals, which include juniper berries (without this piney flavouring, the beverage cannot be called gin), lavender, rose petals, coriander, orange and lemon peel, and several other (secret) ingredients. The most unusual extra flavouring is sustainably harvested winged kelp (*Alaria marginata*), collected in the Juan de Fuca Strait, where it grows naturally in its salty environment. Amanda Swinimer, nicknamed Mermaid of the Pacific, who operates Dakini Tidal Wilds, is the forager who supplies Sheringham with this unique botanical. According to Jason, the seaweed adds a slightly salty taste to the gin that balances the other botanicals. Alcohol by volume is 43 percent.

"We are among Vancouver Island's forests and surrounded by the ocean," says Alayne. "We so enjoyed the blissful feelings we experienced walking along the ocean paths, smelling the fragrance of wild Nootka roses, and hearing the crashing waves. We asked ourselves how we could get these feelings into a glass. The seaweed was key."

Sheringham has also introduced a differently flavoured gin. They describe their Seaside Gin as "a bit floral, with hints of forest, ocean, and citrus, with a bright refreshing taste." Their new version, Kazuki Gin, is more delicate. The botanicals in this gin include juniper, Japanese cherry blossoms, the peel of the Asian yuzu (a citrus fruit), grapefruit, and green tea leaves and green tea flowers from the Cowichan Valley. Alcohol by volume is 43 percent.

Sheringham's fourth spirit, Akvavit, is spiced with dill, caraway, anise, and citrus, and, again, that salty ocean hint of kelp. White wheat and malted barley, both grown in BC, form the base for this spirit. The term *akvavit*, also spelled *aquavit*, derives from the Latin *aqua vitae*, or "water of life." A Barrel Aged Akvavit is also on hand. This spirit has matured in casks that previously stored Sheringham's whiskies. Alcohol by volume for both akvavits is 42 percent.

In 2019, Sheringham released its first whiskies. The first, called Red Fife Whisky, uses BC-grown, heritage Red Fife wheat (Canada's oldest wheat) as its base and is matured in once-used bourbon oak casks, charred deeply to level three. Woodhaven Whisky emerged in 2020, with Jason's creativity and palate in full view. He combined corn, Red Fife wheat, and malted barley as the base and stored the distillate in virgin American oak barrels, also charred to level three. "It has beautiful oak tones," says Jason. "We named it after the side road where we built our first distillery in Shirley, BC." Woodhaven Whisky scored 91 in *Jim Murray's Whisky Bible 2020*.

Sheringham's plans for innovative products haven't stopped there. It partnered with the Stick in the Mud Coffee House, an artisan Sooke coffee shop roasting ethically sourced beans, and created a Coffee Liqueur so delicious I want to drink it directly, not dilute it with coffee. A triple pack containing 100-millilitre bottles of Seaside Gin, Kazuki Gin, and Rhubarb Gin was snapped up as Christmas gifts. The Rhubarb Gin was a one-off and may or may not appear again. A blackberry liqueur may also join the Sheringham family of spirits.

I learned one day at the Sheringham Distillery that the spirits it makes become a base for other people's experimentation. I spoke with Bill Milliken, who has followed Sheringham's progress from the day it opened in Shirley in 2015. He revealed that it's not just distilleries that invent their own specialty libations. "I have two amateur distiller sons-in-law who got me interested in craft distilling," Bill said. "I'm an amateur forager and collect chanterelles and all kinds of berries—salmon, thimble, black, salal, hawthorn, and sloe berries. I find them mostly between Sooke and Port Renfrew. But I won't reveal my special places."

He uses Sheringham's vodka and then infuses it with his foraged harvests. No special equipment is needed. "Let's say I want to infuse winter chanterelles," Bill said. "I place them in

Sheringham's Seaside Gin was named World's Best Contemporary Gin at London's World Gin Awards.

the vodka and wait for the mushrooms' colour to disappear. When they're a ghostly white, I remove them from the alcohol and drink the earthy, woodsy tipple neat. I also make syrups from rhubarb, berries, and mushrooms that blend with infused vodka to make great cocktails. Sheringham supplies the spirits, and I like doing my own thing with them."

AWARDS

Early on, the MacIsaacs began sending their Seaside Gin and Akvavit to various competitions. Just two years after the distillery launched, Seaside Gin won a silver medal at the 2017 San Francisco World Spirits Competition. Sheringham's Akvavit enhanced the distillery's reputation by being named an audience favourite at the BC Distilled festivals in 2017, 2018, and 2019, as well the silver medal at the 2019 San Francisco World Spirits Competition. In 2018, Seaside Gin hit a home run by winning a gold medal at the Canadian Artisan Spirit Competition. "When we won that top medal in a Canada-wide contest, we were amazed and delighted," says Alayne.

They also entered the highly respected World Gin Awards in London. Pitted against the best gins from 26 countries,

Sheringham's Seaside Gin was judged to be the world's best contemporary-style gin.

In the ornate language used to describe alcoholic beverages, the World Gin Awards highlighted Seaside Gin's "spicy, floral, citrus aroma with a hint of white pepper and anise on the palate. Olive, candied fennel seed, light bodied, mild herbal. Slightly longer finish."

Sheringham's senior vice-president, Terence Fitzgerald, represented the company at the London ceremony. The certificate stands proudly on a barrel in the tasting room. Each bottle of Seaside Gin now carries a tiny gold label trumpeting its award. The honour stimulated a flock of press interviews and publications. Many reporters showed up at the door, obliging the company to hire an additional full-time employee.

Sheringham produced about 27,000 litres of spirits in 2018, well within the 50,000-litre limit set by BC's craft distillery rules. But the next year, 2019, showed how awards can stimulate sales and production. The firm distilled 48,000 litres of spirits—creeping up to the limit of 50,000 litres for receiving favourable tax treatment.

I ask Jason if lobbying the BC government to raise the limit for craft distilleries is ongoing. "Indeed, it is," he says. "But so far, they're unwilling to budge."

To me, it sounds counterintuitive. If the goal is to promote BC-grown agricultural products, and to encourage the craft distilleries using these ingredients, the limit is low and should be raised. It would also help fill BC government coffers with more liquor tax revenue.

In March 2020, during the COVID-19 pandemic, the British Columbia government gave temporary authorization to distilleries to begin producing hand sanitizer for donation or for sale. Sheringham joined other craft distillers in adding hand sanitizer to its spirit production and delivering it to first responders. Sheringham called its product Sanette and claims it "kills 99.9 percent of germs."

BEYOND ALCOHOL

Alayne has her finger on the social media pulse and has been following a new trend—enjoying gatherings with non-alcoholic cocktails. Alcohol-free drinks have become popular in the

Sheringham's unique non-alcoholic drink, Lumette.

United Kingdom, and booze-free bars have sprung up in New York. It's explained as "getting out and socializing without the pressure to drink." Or as "conviviality without negative effects." Some millennials define this style as "living healthy and substance-free." The concept has even spread from bars and dance halls to sober events, sober dating, and sober travel. Low-alcohol beer has been around for decades, but now craft spirits are also following this trend.

Sheringham has expanded its horizons and is the first Canadian company to pursue this movement: Alayne has launched a non-alcoholic drink line called Lumette. She describes the product as having the "complex flavours of gin. It's for those who like drinking a cocktail with their family and friends but may serve as designated driver or simply don't imbibe alcohol."

She explains that developing a following in Canada will require education. "Lumette has the same mouth feel as an alcohol cocktail but without the burn. It contains all-natural flavours and premium botanicals, including juniper, grapefruit, orange, and mint. It's handcrafted using our traditional distilling methods but without input of grains, of course. For me, it matters that we provide an equally inspiring non-alcoholic option to cocktail lovers everywhere."

I attended the opening that launched Lumette. The distillery was overflowing with tasters. Several bartenders created multicoloured cocktails with Lumette as the base and then added ingredients such as syrups, fruit, and herbs.

How do the MacIsaacs describe their success? Jason says that when he was cooking, he didn't need fancy pots. What he needed were good ingredients and a good palate. Taste is essential. That's what makes the dish.

"The final product," he says, "comes down to the method, the ingredients, and the person doing it. You can cook an omelette, or you can cook an *omelette*."

TOURS

Sheringham offers a tasting room and tours. For summer and winter hours, visit sheringhamdistillery.com.

FAVOURITE COCKTAILS

NORTHERN HOLIDAY

1½ oz (45 mL) Sheringham Akvavit

½ oz (15 mL) Sheringham Vodka

1 bar spoon Benedictine

2 dashes chocolate bitters

Orange twist

In a mixing glass combine all ingredients, add ice, and stir. Strain into a chilled cocktail coupe and garnish with an orange twist.

GIN MARTINI

1½ oz (45 mL) Sheringham Seaside Gin

¼ oz (7 mL) Lillet

1 tsp (5 mL) olive brine

Olives for garnish

Pour into a martini glass and garnish with olives.

VODKA HONEY OLD-FASHIONED

Zest of lemon

2 oz (60 mL) Sheringham Vodka

½ oz (15 mL) honey syrup (1:1 honey and hot water)

2 dashes orange bitters

2 dashes tobacco leaf bitters

In a rocks glass add a cheek of lemon zest, the vodka, and the honey syrup. Muddle the lemon zest to release the oils. Add the bitters and ice. Stir and strain into an ice-filled rocks glass. Garnish with fresh zest of lemon.

GIN CAIPIRINHA

½ lime, cut into quarters

2 Tbsp (30 mL) honey

1½ oz (45 mL) Sheringham Seaside Gin

Combine the lime wedges and the honey in a rocks glass. Muddle to release the juices. Fill the glass with ice and add the Seaside Gin. Transfer the contents into a cocktail shaker and shake vigorously. Dump back into the original rocks glass.

2
MACALONEY'S CALEDONIAN DISTILLERY & TWA DOGS BREWERY

GRAEME MACALONEY, OWNER AND DISTILLER

761 ENTERPRISE CRESCENT

VICTORIA, BC V8Z 6P7

778-401-0410

INFO@MACALONEYDISTILLERS.COM

VICTORIACALEDONIAN.COM

LATITUDE 48.484740, LONGITUDE -123.387090

FOR GRAEME MACALONEY, WHISKY IS BRED IN THE bone. He's the genuine article, born in the village of Gartcosh, Scotland, a few kilometres east of Glasgow in North Lanarkshire, a part of the world where the art of whisky making is legendary. He wears his ancestral Cameron tartan kilt complete with sporran and white knee socks. His Scottish accent evokes visions of heather, thistle, and bagpipes. "As a student, I had a summer job at the Black and White Scotch distillery, and I fell in love with *Uisge Beatha*, Gaelic for 'water of life,'" he tells me in his tasting room, which doubles as a pub, at Macaloney's Caledonian Distillery (the name recently changed from Victoria Caledonian Distillery). "I've always had the idea that someday I'd have a distillery of my own.

"My ancestry goes back 10 generations to the Isle of Islay," he continues. "That's seven great-grandfathers back. He was an *Ileach*, as the island people call themselves."

Islay is the southernmost island of the Inner Hebrides and one of the five Scotch whisky regions. The 620-square-kilo-metre island is renowned for such distilleries as Laphroaig, Lagavulin, and Ardbeg that flavour their whiskies with the smoke of burning peat, which they hand cut from the local bogs. "The Isle of Islay is to peated-whisky lovers what Rome is to Catholics, Mecca is to Muslims," says Graeme.

THE ISLE OF ISLAY INFLUENCE

Graeme's Islay heritage is part of his motivation to design distinct whiskies not usually produced in Canada. Classic single malt and Irish-style whiskeys have been maturing in the casks in his spacious warehouse, and he launched the first Canadian peat-smoked whiskies in 2020. "I call our peated whisky Islay

bred and inspired," he says. "This whisky, named Peated Mac na Braiche, appeals to the so-called peat heads." (*Mac na braiche* literally means "son of the malt," but in Scotland the term is commonly used to describe single malt.)

Peat smoke produces chemicals called phenols, which are absorbed by malted barley. Graeme hands me two glasses filled with tawny-coloured grain grown in BC. "This one is regular malted and dried barley," he says. "You can see the little sprouts when the barley germinated. But the other glass contains barley that's been bathed in peat smoke. It's popcorn for peat heads."

Graeme Macaloney with his Forsyths pot stills.

I sniff and taste a few kernels from the first glass. It's crunchy. "I think this would fit well into my homemade granola," I say. The second grain is equally crispy, but its scent and taste leads me to fantasize I'm visiting Islay.

The longer the grain is infused with peat smoke, the stronger the spirit's smokiness. The strength of the "peatiness" is measured in parts per million (ppm). To ensure his peated barley is competitive with Islay and Scotch products, Graeme sent some of his smoky grain to a Scottish lab. The results showed that at the barley stage (before distillation), his smoke content measured 54 ppm, similar to Ardbeg's 54 ppm but higher than Laphroaig's 40–50 ppm, while Bowmore enters the fray at 22 ppm for its standard product. "That measurement does not remain constant though," Graeme adds. "The final flavour depth the whisky will unveil at maturity will have been influenced by the copper distillation process, the type of cask in which the spirit has been stored, and for how long it's been squirrelled away."

Graeme visited Islay twice and spent time at the Laphroaig distillery, observing how they smoke their barley. "I am applying what I learned to some of our Caledonian malt whiskies, making us among the first in North America to produce whisky using local barley, peat-smoking it on-site, and making it on a commercial scale," he says. He projects that within five years the products that are laid down and maturing now will be sold around the world.

He leads me outside his 17,000-square-foot facility to show me how Caledonian smokes its barley. On the way, we walk between his huge stores of barley, supplied by British Columbia's Gambrinus Malting, tightly bound in heavy white plastic sacks. Each sack, lounging on a pallet, weighs 1,000 kilograms. We also pass a gristmill, which breaks down the barley kernels and exposes more of the grain's starch. It's the milled barley that enters the mashing tanks.

The soaker/smoker is custom-made of sturdy, silvery aluminum. "My cousin-in-law in Alberta built the smoker to my design," he says, while rolling back the container's cover from its supporting frames. "We've nicknamed it Sir Mike in honour of our master distiller, Mike Nicolson. Mike used to distill at Lagavulin Distillery on Islay, among other spirit makers."

Graeme clambers into the smoker and stands on its corrugated, perforated floor, which easily carries his weight. The smoker holds 2,000 kilograms—two of those sacks of Gambrinus's malted barley, which become heavier as they soak overnight. After excess water is drained, the peat, composed of slowly decayed plant materials, smoulders in an external wood stove; the smoke is piped into the smoker through a valve. A blower fan circulates and

Graeme Macaloney standing inside his peat soaker/smoker.

distributes the smoke evenly. The process takes a couple of days, then the smoked barley is dried until only 4–5 percent moisture remains.

During the next steps, the milled peaty barley is loaded into stainless steel mash tuns, where water and heat turn the bar-ley's sugars into alcohol.

Macaloney's Caledonian Distillery's soaker/smoker in action.

Electrically powered paddles stir the mash, ensuring the malt grist is thoroughly wetted. Yeast is added to the resulting liquid, called wort, which ferments for two or three days to become wash, which is then distilled twice in Caledonian's twin pot stills. A new make, or "prelude to Mac na Braiche," was sold after a one year's maturation. (New make is whisky that hasn't yet met the three-year maturation requirement.) Its "adult" versions—lightly peated, moderately peated, and heavily peated single malt—are aging gracefully and will launch in 2022.

"Who supplies your peat?" I ask Graeme. "You don't import it from Islay, do you?"

He grins and answers, "No. It comes from the Olympic Peninsula, just

Stirring the cooking mash.

across Juan de Fuca Strait." He says the Washington-based peat still makes it part of the regional "terroir," a French term that explains how locality, climate, weather, topography, and soil types influence the flavour profile of each batch of alcoholic beverages.

"You see," he says, "when Indigenous people lived on what is now Vancouver Island and Washington State, there were no international borders. This was all their territory. When Europeans and the Hudson's Bay Company arrived and took their lands, they called this area New Caledonia, but boundaries were unclear. People moved easily through the regions that are now parts of Canada and the United States. But our climate and weather, salt water, clean water, pure air, rains, and mountains are all part of the same Pacific Ocean forces and tectonic plates. Our borders are artificial. That's why Olympic peat is part of the greater terroir."

He then explains he named his distillery Caledonian for this recent, as well as ancient, history. Caledonia was the Latin name for Scotland when Roman legions occupied the British Isles in the early parts of the first millennium. The term is still used in Scottish poetry. The name is also reflected in the Caledonian Canal, the waterway that connects Inverness, on Scotland's northeast coast, with the country's west coast, thereby creating a shipping shortcut.

DESIGNING THE WHISKIES

Not everyone is fond of the earthy taste of peated whisky, thus Graeme has laid up several classic types of whisky as well. When he was planning to distill the first batches more than four years ago, he asked whisky maturation expert Dr. Jim Swan, who's been called the "Einstein of whiskies" and "the ultimate whisky troubleshooter," to help him design the best products possible. According to the Whisky Foundation, Swan "was very much a behind-the-scenes man, using his lifetime of experience—and staggering amount of knowledge—to help young distilleries produce great quality whisky very quickly."

"Jim Swan was famous for inventing the genre of 'finished' whiskies with the launch of the Glenmorangie series," says Graeme. "He also took Kavalan's Taiwanese whisky from nowhere to winning the world's best single malt in the 2015 World Whiskies Awards, despite it being just five years old."

Before Swan died in 2017, he consulted with Caledonian. "We were his second-to-last project and the only Canadian company to benefit from his expertise," says Graeme. "Along with our master distiller, Mike Nicolson, Swan and I met in August 2016, and we designed our classic whisky processes in the Scottish tradition. He optimized our processes and our raw 'new make' spirits grew better with each batch. Our goal was to develop whiskies that would not only mature quickly but also refashion Canadian barley into ultra-quality single malt whiskies for international export beyond North American shores." (To legally be called single malt, a whisky must be distilled at a single distillery in a copper pot still using only malted barley, yeast, and water. It must then be aged in an oak cask for at least three years and a day and be bottled at no less than 40 percent alcohol by volume.)

Caledonian followed Swan's recommendations, and when he tasted the early batches, he said it was the best, fruitiest whisky he'd tasted anywhere. The testimonial from this expert gave Graeme the "intestinal fortitude" to send a bottle to the World Whiskies Awards in London.

The gamble paid off. In 2019, the whisky was named Best Canadian New Make, which placed it in the top two in the world and left a living legacy for Dr. Swan.

Mike Nicolson was the other specialist Graeme recruited. "Mike is a production guru and a master distiller," he says. "He has a long pedigree working in 18 Scottish distilleries belonging to Diageo, an alcoholic beverage conglomerate that owns more than 200 trademarks, including such well-known brands as Crown Royal, Johnny Walker, Baileys, Guinness, and Captain Morgan."

Swan's recommendations for making excellent-quality whisky over a relatively short maturation time have continued to bear fruit. "We extended what we learned from him to our peated whisky products and also laid down our first Irish-style whiskey as well," says Graeme. "I combined the knowledge Swan gave us by learning more at Islay's Laphroaig distillery and later attending the Irish Whiskey Academy in Cork on the grounds of the Old and New Midleton Distilleries."

Graeme also likes Irish-style whiskeys, which are made with a blend of malted and unmalted barley. The Irish part again harks back to his ancestry. "In the early Middle Ages, my Scottish clan emigrated from Ireland," he says. The Irish-style whiskey has been ripening in its casks. It's a triple-distilled spirit that reaches 85 percent alcohol; the mix of both malted and unmalted barley creates a drink that is grainier, with a biscuity, creamy mouth feel.

Caledonian began selling the Irish-style new make, named Oaken Poitín, at one-and-a-half-year maturation in mid-2020 and plans to launch the mature whiskey in January 2022.

Inside Caledonian's distilling room.

THE DISTILLING PROCESS

Graeme tours me through his still house, a huge space where a bank of lofty stainless steel mash tuns and beer fermenters dominate one wall. (More about the brewery later.) The yeasty aroma of the fermenting barley combined with the "angel's share" (the evaporation of spirits through their wood casks) evokes fantasies of future enjoyment. In one corner of the vast room, Caledonian's bottling station fills many different kinds of beer into its glass containers. The central portion of the room is capacious enough to host dinners, whisky launches, events, and parties. Facing the mash tuns and fermenters, two giant, hand-hammered copper pot stills occupy a good portion of a raised platform. They look like gigantic Hershey's Kisses with attached piping. Graeme ordered the two tall (4.8-metre) copper stills—5,500-litre and 3,600-litre, respectively—from Forsyths, a Scottish company that began building its handmade stills in 1895. It customizes its stills to client specifications. Caledonian uses steam to heat radiators that bring the wash to the alcohol boiling point.

The copper in the stills distributes heat evenly and also changes the alcohol's taste profile. The yeast that fuelled the wort's fermentation produces sulphur compounds that can add a bitter taste to whisky. But during distillation, the sulphur attaches to the copper stills' innards, thereby producing hydrogen sulphide and copper sulphate. These chemicals stick to the copper walls and are left behind as the spirit exits the still. "We double-distill our spirits, and each time the alcohol continuously touches the copper walls, it becomes a fruitier, smoother, and lighter whisky," says Graeme. "The stills' walls build up a patina over time that gives character to our whiskies."

The stills' distillate, or ethanol, runs into Caledonian's spirit safe—a padlocked, rectangular, glass and metal device—which measures temperature and the density of the alcohol by volume.

The spirit safe originated after the 1823 Excise Act in Scotland, which stipulated how much the taxman could collect based on the safe's alcohol by volume. Whisky levies became so important to government revenues ("a total cash cow," says Graeme) that excise men inhabited houses built on the distilleries' premises to ensure no whisky left without payment of the levies that filled state coffers.

Today, spirit safes are not required in Canada, but Caledonian chose to install one. Its modern controls and a hydrometer cut the distillate and direct the heads, hearts, and tails to various stainless steel vats. Only Graeme has the padlock's key. "The tax collector doesn't come around to check the safe today," he says, "but we have followed the requirement to have our spirit safe equipment calibrated in a certified lab to ensure our alcohol-by-volume measurements are accurate."

From the spirit safe, the clear ethanol is channelled into a stainless steel receiver, while the heads and tails are stored in another container. "When we distill the next batch, we add the heads and tails to the wash. They are constantly recycled. As you know, the Scots are known for their thrift. Basically, they're too cheap to throw anything out. We follow that tradition."

During the second distillation, Caledonian collects the ethanol's hearts, and they're piped into a whisky tank called the final spirit receiver, where the alcohol content is adjusted to 63.5 percent. From there, the alcohol is pumped into individual casks, where it mellows and matures. When it's of age, however, the alcohol level will be lower. That's due to an annual up to 2 percent evaporation through the barrel's porous wood. That loss is known in the industry as the "angel's share."

When the whisky is mature, it's bottled and the alcohol content is again adjusted. The final Caledonian products contain 46 percent alcohol by volume—92 proof. By law, whisky must contain 40 percent alcohol, but Graeme says that's "too thin, too watery" for his taste.

THE FIRST MATURE CLASSIC WHISKIES

Caledonian launched its inaugural batch of classic whisky in early 2020, after it had matured for three years, the age at which spirits legally become whisky. The term *Scotch* can be used only by whiskies produced in Scotland. Thus Caledonian created this "correct" tag line for its whiskies: "Traditionally made by Scots."

The release has two different expressions, each influenced by the casks in which it matured. "Whisky must be stored in oak casks, no other wood," Graeme says. "But what changes the flavour of each cask's contents is what it contained before we filled it with our whisky. Wood makes the whisky."

Caledonian's Glenloy brand uses four types of casks that once stored different alcoholic beverages: bourbon, red wine, and two kinds of sherry. Oloroso is a dry sherry made in Andalusia, Spain, which has matured using oxidative aging. The other, Pedro Ximénez, also produced in Spain, is an intensely sweet, dark sherry. Each of the four types of casks creates a whisky with an individual flavour profile.

Invermallie, the other Caledonian classic whisky style, consists of limited-release, single-cask expressions. Each cask contains between 250 and 350 bottles, depending on the angel's share. The first type has matured in casks formerly containing a fortified sweet Muscatel. The second release presents whisky matured in casks that once contained sherry. "This style has its own following," explains Graeme, his blue eyes crinkling. "When you drink it, it seems as if a sherry bomb explodes in your mouth, evoking tastes of chocolate cake and plum pudding."

The third single-cask release matured in red wine barriques whose interior walls have been recharred.

The recharred casks have been treated with the STR method, which stands for shaving, toasting, and recharring, another process pioneered by Jim Swan. First, the casks' insides are shaved to expose new oak; then, hot flames toast and char the wood, which opens the wood up and exposes the spirit to a different environment that maximizes flavour extraction. Charred interiors are a deep black, and the sugars from the caramelized wood not only bestow sweet, caramel flavours but also lend the whisky a rich, deep colour. "We employ charred and/or previously used casks, as the wood in virgin casks overpowers the whisky," says Graeme.

To make sure he'd choose the right wood casks, Graeme went to cooperages in Portugal, Spain, and the US state of Kentucky. He points out that not only the previous contents of casks influence the spirit's eventual flavour, "but even the wood in each cask can affect the final product. You can put the same spirit in the same type of oak penetrated earlier by the same alcohol, yet end up with a different taste. The oaken staves can be manufactured from different trees, or from a different part of a tree. That's why connoisseurs love single-cask products. Each barrel and its bottled product will have its own personality."

A stave from a charred cask that flavours whisky.

THE BUSINESS PLAN

Making whisky is not only labour intensive but also a costly undertaking. A property large enough and with high enough ceilings to house stills, mash tuns, fermenters, barley, and casks, along with a tasting room and product displays, may require a warehouse in a light-industrial area or in a rural zone. The essential equipment can run into the millions of dollars. The three years that whisky takes to mature produce little cash flow.

To finance Caledonian, Graeme developed a series of innovative arrangements. It seems that, even unintentionally, he prepared for decades to launch his distillery/brewery. At first glance, it might appear his previous studies and jobs were unrelated to his present enterprise, but retrospectively, it's clear educational and industrial experiences have abetted his desire to develop a successful business based on fermentation.

He studied microbiology at the University of Strathclyde in Glasgow and then earned a master's degree in biochemical engineering at University College London. He returned to Strathclyde for a PhD in microbiology or, he says with a chuckle, "fermentation."

"After graduation, when I applied for fermentation-related jobs in the UK," he says, "I kept being told I was overqualified." He ended up in pharmaceuticals, working for Pfizer and Eli Lilly in their antibiotics divisions. "Some people don't realize that antibiotic production depends on a heavy dose of fermentation technology, similar to that of beer brewing and liquor production."

In 1989, Graeme immigrated to Canada, having found a position at the Alberta Research Council's pilot fermentation plant, which provides manufacturing support and testing to outside companies. He also discovered the joys of Canada's outdoors and judged the quality of life to be better than that in the UK. "While at the Research Council, I learned about biotech companies and start-ups using our services," he says. "Many had found innovative ways to fund their enterprises with equity financing and angel investors. I knew that a start-up distillery needed major investment but would have low revenues while the alcohol matures. Those innovators led me to take the plunge. I started looking for ways to fund Caledonian."

He found several inventive ways to do so. First, using the Gaelic slogan "Ceud mile fàilte gu an clann," or "A hundred thousand welcomes to our clan," he enticed more than 325 founder-owner-investors to believe in his vision, raising more than $7 million in equity financing.

Second, he combined his distillery dreams with a brewery, calling it Twa Dogs, after the long poem by Robert Burns. "People are often surprised to learn that a distillery is essentially a brewery with two copper pot stills attached at the end," he says. "Whisky is beer without the hops that's been distilled twice. And the combination of brewery and distillery allows us to develop crossover products."

Beer can be produced quickly, and Caledonian has created a group of unfiltered specialty beers that have attracted a faithful following and a steady cash flow. Graeme continues to invent catchy names for the craft beers, all with a whiff of humour, including Hazy Mist New England IPA, Life and Liberty Pale Ale, Holy Willie's Robust Porter, and Sink or Swim Belgian Wit. His beers include the pelletized flowers of hops, giving a bitterness and floral tastes to the beverage. "Our Twa Dogs beer drinkers are very demanding and always looking for new tastes, so we make a new beer about every six weeks," says Graeme, "as well as seasonal and brewer's specials." Caledonian also uses some of its peated malt barley to make special "smoky" beers.

Third, Caledonian created a series of blended malt whiskies selected from 12 Scottish distilleries. Called the Macaloney's Twa Cask Series, the three individual blends provide a reasonably priced introduction to malt Scotch whisky. To encourage buyers, Caledonian creates custom labels with the purchaser's name, the name of a family member or friend, or a company logo. These can be ordered in advance at the Caledonian website. Again, the sale of these Scotches added to the company's cash flow early on, but as the distillery's own spirits matured, these blends were phased out.

Graeme also asked Agriculture and Agri-Food Canada for a $2.4 million interest-free loan, demonstrating how a renewable commodity, Canadian barley, could be transformed into "ultra-quality, single malt whiskies for the international export market." The federal department, noting Caledonian's other revenue streams and appreciating Jim Swan's endorsement of the new-make Caledonian whiskies, agreed to the loan.

As an added marketing feature, Graeme invited individuals to buy their own cask. More than 170 people signed up for the cask program and designed their own whisky experience by choosing different whisky expressions and their own kind of cask. It's an opportunity for whisky lovers to own a unique spirit, literally calling the shots. Casks contain either 30 or 200 litres, while a red wine barrique—the standard wine cask—carries 225 litres. "It's a bundle of fun," says Graeme. "While the spirit is sleeping and aging, the purchasers can visit their cask, smell the angel's share, and get a taste of how their whisky is progressing. When the maturation date arrives, they can hand bottle their spirits, apply their own label, and take some great memories and world-class whisky home. Some people exchange a few of their bottles with the other cask owners."

It costs about $3,000 to own your own 30-litre cask, so at $100 per litre bottle, it's not an inexpensive leisure pursuit. But it's great fun and, most of all, truly unique. No other person in the world has the same distinctively flavoured whisky!

Not only individuals bought a cask. The Grand Lodge of British Columbia, for example, bought two, which it will auction off as a fundraiser. It may raise as much as $25,000 per cask.

Finally, Graeme turned to a crowdfunding campaign, explaining via the FrontFundr website how people's investment will help Caledonian to take its "great whiskies global and in the process help the Canadian craft whisky sector win international recognition." The minimum buy-in was $500, and for an investment of $5,000, investors could place it in their registered retirement savings plan or tax-free savings account. The goal of raising $500,000 was exceeded by nearly $200,000. Caledonian now has another group of 175 enthusiastic investors who will spread the word about Caledonian's spirits and beers and, of course, hope for a hefty return on investment. Given that the crowdfunding was so successful in recruiting passionate consumers, Graeme plans to launch a campaign each year.

Caledonian offers benefits to its investors and crowdfunders, with perks increasing depending on the investment level. The perks may include free, branded swag such as toques, T-shirts, jackets, free tours, lifetime happy-birthday pints, and various discounts on whisky tastings and the three-day Caley Brewing and Distilling Academy.

How will crowdfunding proceeds be used by Caledonian? The company will focus on laying down more whisky stocks and expanding whisky sales globally.

"Caledonian whisky is more than a passion for me," Graeme concludes. "It creates connections with other people. Everyone who comes to our facility is smiling. It's a very good business to be in."

AWARDS

Caledonian has earned several top awards for its whiskies. At the 2020 World Whiskies Awards in London, Invermallie (matured in an STR red wine barrique single cask) was named Best Canadian Single Cask Single Malt. Graeme and his team were especially pleased to win Best Canadian New Make for their Peated Clearach. Moreover, at the 2020 San Francisco World Spirits Competition, Caledonian won gold for three of its whiskies: Twa Cask Islay, Twa Cask Speyside, and Twa Cask Highland. All three of these were finished in STR red wine barriques. Twa Cask Islay scored 93 points in *Jim Murray's Whisky Bible 2020*.

Caledonian's peated whisky with its gold medal.

TOURS AND EVENTS

Caledonian's business plan includes bringing as many people to the premises as possible. "Tourism is a core part of our business," says Graeme. Interactive tours are offered to locals and visitors—it's an enjoyable way to learn the culture of beer brewing and whisky distilling while also tasting the tipples produced on-site. The tour includes a short history on the making of Scottish and Irish whiskies.

Graeme also plans to create a Northwest whisky trail, which will include visits to a few distilleries in Washington and collaboration with the *Victoria Clipper* and the *Coho* to bring passengers to Vancouver Island. A stop at Caledonian will then lead to a trip "up Island" to Shelter Point Distillery near Campbell River.

With a Scotsman in charge, it's natural that Caledonian hosts an annual Robbie Burns dinner, complete with bagpipers, haggis, and, of course, some very fine drams of whisky made in the adjacent copper stills. I attended the 2020 Robbie Burns dinner, held between the Forsyths stills and the fermentation tanks. The group of whisky lovers were greeted with a pint of Twa Dogs lager, and with two pipers and a drummer from the Royal Canadian Air Force. While the bagpipes skirled, Graeme pierced the haggis, which we ate along with tatties and neeps. Kilt-clad staff members took turns reciting Robbie Burns poems, while we celebrators quaffed four different whisky expressions. As his poems attest, Burns loved a good party, with food, drink, music, and poetry. Caledonian put on a proper salute to the Scottish bard and his national drink.

If you want to gain a more detailed knowledge of liquor production, Caledonian has engaged the Statera Academy to offer the Wine & Spirit Education Trust's WSET Level 1 Award in Spirits course, a hands-on program described as "a beginner level introduction to spirits for those starting a career in the industry or pursuing an interest in spirits."

FAVOURITE COCKTAIL

THE SMOKY MAC ROY

1½ oz (45 mL) Peated Mac na Braiche
1 oz (30 mL) sweet vermouth
1 dash Angostura Bitters

Put the ingredients in a cocktail mixer full of ice and stir—don't shake (we aren't James Bond). Strain and pour into a martini glass. May be garnished with a cherry.

3
MOON
DISTILLERY

CLAY POTTER, CO-OWNER AND DISTILLER

350A BAY STREET

VICTORIA, BC V8T 1P7

250-385-0315

MOONDISTILLERY@MOONUNDERWATER.CA

MOONDISTILLERY.CA

LATITUDE 48.435130, LONGITUDE -123.375490

THE **MOON** BREWPUB

350

Clay Potter by his Moon brewery, distillery, and pub.

CLAYTON POTTER, WHO BREWS BEER AND DISTILLS spirits at Moon Distillery, learned to appreciate beer early in his young life. Every Friday night, his mum, Anne Farmer-Ash, brought home a six-pack—each beer a different European brand and flavour. Mother and son would share a beer taste test. Meanwhile, Clay's stepfather, Steve Ash, operated a metal shop next door to Phillips Brewery when that firm first launched in Esquimalt. He became acquainted with the owner, Matt Phillips, and watched the company grow from a tiny craft brewery to the prime craft beer producer in British Columbia. "We loved their beers," says Clay. "And my stepdad was there when welding and other metalwork were needed."

Clay enrolled at the University of Victoria (UVic), majoring in microbiology and intending to go to medical school. During a co-op work term, he started working at Lighthouse Brewery in Esquimalt. "I set up a testing lab for them," Clay says. "But the brewmaster left to set up his own company. So another young guy, Dan Murphy, and I were both promoted to brewer. We had home brewed together in the past, so we were the only two people there with any experience. I was only 20 but worked full-time. Heady days. I also eventually earned my UVic microbiology degree."

Clay's ambition to become a physician waned as he grew ever more enamoured of the brewing process. "I fell in love with the industry," he says. He spent more than three years at Lighthouse performing tasks such as fermenting, brewing, filtering, and packaging. He set up a quality-control lab and also developed a yeast-management system that optimizes the concentration and oxygenation rates for different types of yeast strains. Obviously, the microbiology studies had an applied effect.

But he felt he needed more education specifically devoted to the art and science of brewing and distilling. So he enrolled at Heriot-Watt University in Edinburgh. The coursework delivered a diploma in distilling and brewing, but to earn a master of science required a thesis. Clay chose a scientific topic: the microbiology of beer in on-trade. On-trade?

"It refers to the equipment used in selling beer in a bar, pub, or restaurant," Clay explains. "I used polymerase chain reactions to study the various organisms, such as bacteria and yeasts, that can grow inside beer hoses and dispensers. These can spoil the beer. Let me add, though, that no organisms in beer can survive in humans. The environments, like the pH, alcohol, hops, and temperature are just too different. Thus the organisms in beer don't make imbibers sick. What makes people sick is almost always due to beer's regular old poison—alcohol. What the organisms do cause are off-flavours that ruin the beer's taste. That's what we usually worry about in the on-trade."

Clay's studies tried to determine if it was possible to create a quick method to detect whether contamination was taking place. "I went to a lot of pubs in Edinburgh and surroundings to do 'research.' Craft beer breweries were just starting. I tested what organisms grew, how often they grew, and thus when beer lines needed to be cleaned. My research was paid for by 3M Pharma, who wanted to develop beer-spoiler testing technology."

Clay clarifies that his research conducted in 2009 has been superseded. Today's testing for contaminants in hoses and taps is easy: take a swab and plug it into a machine that then provides a readout of any lurking organisms. "Cleanliness," he says, "is essential in every part of a brewery and beer-dispensing equipment."

After earning his master's degree at Heriot-Watt University, Clay returned to Canada and took a job at Turning Point Brewery in Vancouver. "This brewery was also making ready-to-drink beverages then. These canned drinks are spirit based but have a lower alcohol level than either wine or spirits."

A FAMILY AFFAIR

One day a friend wrote Clay's stepfather that he'd spotted an advertisement: the Moon Under Water Brewery and Taphouse in downtown Victoria was for sale. It was an opportunity that changed the lives of the entire family. "My mother visited the owners and learned they were ready to retire," says Clay. "The pub needed upgrading, and it was more than they wanted to undertake. My mother, stepfather, and I pooled our resources. I moved back to Victoria, sold a house, and all three of us maxed out our credit cards. We invested every last penny we could lay our hands on."

Today, the three co-owners each have their niche. Anne runs the office, manages the finances, and oversees the restaurant; Clay and his crew brew beer and distill spirits; and Steve ensures all the equipment works, while also pitching in whenever needed. Clay's partner, Julia Livingston, joined the company as the marketing manager.

The family trio kept the Moon name, refurbished the pub, and focused on brewing German-style beers, continually devising new flavours. But after being in business for about five years, growth slowed. When the family launched the business in 2012, about 50 craft breweries had opened their doors in British Columbia, but by 2017, that number had quadrupled and was still growing. "We had a lot more breweries, but the pie wasn't getting bigger," Clay notes. "The ready-to-drink market was also expanding and cut into the craft beer market." Studies confirm this trend. According to the *Globe and Mail*, "nationwide, the number [of craft breweries] more than doubled in the last five years to 972 breweries in 2019, up from 383 in 2015. . . . Another 200 breweries are expected to open over the next year, according to the Canadian Craft Brewers Association."

THE MOON DISTILLERY

Clay opted to diversify; he dusted off his distillery credentials and started looking for a commercial still. When a property next to the brewery and pub became available, he and his family partners acquired it so they would have room for both the

The Genio still in the Moon distilling room.

distillery and a spirit-tasting room and cocktail lounge. Clay and Steve had already been experimenting with distilling small batches of rye, whisky, and rum in a 30-litre, all-copper still.

While the new premises were being converted to a spirit-tasting room, Clay bought a larger still. It's a Genio, a 500-litre still manufactured in Sieluń, Poland. It looks different from most stills—it has a black insulating outside cover, and the pot's interior is lined with stainless steel. "It's designed for vodka," says Clay, "but it can bypass the plates to make whisky. I can add a gin column two feet tall that I fill with copper coils. That's the copper contact needed to make whisky. I bought this adaptable still because it required a lower investment."

Moon formally started the distillery in December 2017. Opening the tasting room, however, took a while. "The provincial and the federal licences to distill and open a tasting room were easy to obtain, just paperwork," says Clay. "It was the Victoria permit that slowed everything down. It seemed to me the City of Victoria staff had seen old movies with moonshine stills blowing up, and they made unnecessary requirements such as blast walls and sprinkling systems that would have cost hundreds of thousands. We simply didn't have the funds. As they didn't know a thing about distilling, I had to show the city the premises were safe. In the end, after 18 months of wrangling, I had to hire three architects to sign off that the tasting room was safe and we should have a licence. We finally opened in March 2019."

While awaiting the tasting room licence, Clay used his valid distilling licence to make whiskies and squirrelled them away to mature. He also made a single barrel of rye whisky from 40 percent unmalted rye and 60 percent malted barley. The grains are supplied by South Peace Grain in Dawson Creek, BC.

Copper coils in the column remove sulphides from the wash.

His Scottish-inspired whisky uses 100 percent Vancouver Island–grown malted barley, delivered by

Phillips Brewing & Malting. It's mashed again in one of Moon's mash tuns, and the wash is distilled through the Genio still, its column packed with copper coils to give it the required copper contact. "It mimics a copper still," Clay says. "It's a poor man's copper still." The second run is distilled through the smaller, all-copper still.

Clay has acquired 60 diverse casks that once held bourbon, Burgundy, Bordeaux, and port. His whiskies are maturing in these casks, which are tucked away in the distillery's nooks. Some of the casks once devoted to fruited and sour beers are now doing double duty in the distillery. He plans the first launch of this gracefully aging spirit for the spring of 2021. As the casks and their previous contents are different, the whiskies will be blended to achieve optimum flavour, mouth feel, and aftertaste.

Moon Distillery has also created a single malt whisky project through which customers can purchase a five-litre cask, with their name custom engraved. "It's made with an all-barley, double-distilled base," says Clay, "and we placed it in fresh, medium-toast American oak casks.

Because the casks are small, more of the whisky is exposed to its wood envelope so it doesn't quite need the usual three-year maturation. But the cask's small size also increases the angel's share [evaporation] up to seven percent. I mist the casks regularly to minimize the loss. We also put 60 percent alcohol by volume into the casks to make up for the evaporation."

Moon sold a bunch of the five-litre casks. They not only proved popular

Clay Potter with a five-litre whisky cask.

with individual whisky lovers but also have served as wedding or retirement presents. They cost $375 a cask and deliver 10 bottles containing 40 percent alcohol by volume.

Once the tasting room licence was obtained, Clay created a fleet of flavoured vodkas and gins. He says that gin has seen a revival, is the best seller at the various farmer and craft markets, and is now the "in" cocktail spirit. He and bartender Cham Erikson are continuously experimenting with new cocktail recipes. In 2020, Moon added several new flavoured gins and discontinued some flavoured vodkas. Gin flights—featuring four drinks containing Moon's flavoured gin infusions—are also on the cocktail menu. "We are evolving with the changing tastes in cocktails," says Clay.

Ready for cocktail hour.

One of the Moon tasting room's advantages is that customers can order off the full bill of fare from the pub located right next door. Pairing food with cocktails is a capital idea for people who must drive home after their evening out. "Our premises now do triple duty," says Clay. "The brewery's beers, the distillery's spirits, and the restaurant's food all work together." For the owners, however, these integrated services tend to demand they work seven days a week.

Clay intends to grow his whisky batches over the coming years, and to continue to build on the cocktail business. The planned summer outdoor patio with its view of Victoria Harbour will also attract more customers.

MOON DISTILLERY'S PRODUCTS

Moon's Pure Grain Vodka is made from 60 percent Vancouver Island–grown barley and 40 percent raw wheat from BC's South Peace Grain. The double-distilled product leaves the still as pure ethanol and provides the base for all the flavoured vodkas Moon produces. Clay then filters the vodka through activated charcoal six times to remove any impurities and any strong barley flavours. All of Moon's pure and flavoured vodkas contain 40 percent alcohol by volume.

Orange Vodka is pure grain vodka infused with sweet orange peel from Curaçao, which produces a strong citrus flavour and bright tangerine colour. It's always available and is Moon's most popular flavoured vodka. A variation on this spirit is Chocolate Orange Vodka.

Espresso Vodka teams Moon's vodka with freshly ground espresso beans from Victoria's Oughtred Coffee & Tea, another family-run business established 40 years ago. Oughtred sources its beans from around the world and won *Roast Magazine*'s 2018 Macro Roaster of the Year Award. To make the Espresso Vodka, Clay cold-extracts the beans' flavour by first grinding them and then steeping them in chilled pure grain vodka for 36 hours.

Shaft Liqueur is the distillery's twist on Victoria's famous Shaft Cocktail shooter. Bartender Cham Erikson told me how Moon's version of the Shaft is made. "We start with our Shaft Liqueur and add cold-brew coarse-ground Oughtred espresso beans that have soaked in a cheesecloth bag in 4°C [39°F] water for 14 hours, add a dab of cream and a dab of honey, then pour the concoction over ice. It's one of the favourite cocktails in the distillery's tasting lounge."

For the gin, Clay starts with a barley and wheat wash, performs a stripping run to remove water, yeast, and sediments, and then completes a second run to concentrate the alcohol. The final distillation takes place in the all-copper still with the botanicals, which include local juniper berries, orange peel, lemon peel, grapefruit peel, and coriander. Called Citrus Gin, it is made in small batches distilled in Moon's copper pot still. Citrus Gin is the base for the other flavoured gins. It's mostly sold online and on-site.

The Naked Stroll in the Forest Gin is very popular. It contains locally foraged botanicals including juniper berries, lavender, rose petals, spruce tips, pine tips, and chamomile. "They are gathered for us by forager Kalynka Cherkosh," says Clay. "She's great with flavours. Since the botanicals are foraged, they tend to be a bit different and each batch of gin is therefore unique."

Clay prepares Moon's liqueurs from a vodka base when the blueberries, raspberries, loganberries, and strawberries are ripe. They may vary annually according to what fruit is available. These popular fruit-flavoured liqueurs are mixed with various cocktail ingredients and served in the tasting room.

Other spirits get added to the menu from time to time. Some are seasonal; some are experimental. In 2020, the bill of fare included a candy cane schnapps, shiso vodka (shiso is in the mint family), and sloe gin infused with wild sloe berries. A honey and oats vodka is steeped with local honey and whole-grain oats.

In addition, last year, because of the expanding popularity of gin, Moon added a blueberry gin to its staple spirits, as well as seasonal gins, including raspberry gin, strawberry gin, and spruce tip gin, the latter infused with the piney fragrance of the tips as they emerge from the trees' winter sleep.

AWARDS

So far, Moon Distillery has not sent in any of its spirits to competitions. "We have received many beer awards," says Clay. "But for spirits it's expensive to enter contests, and we have to pay for packaging and freight. There may be duties and taxes in other countries. We're doing okay locally, and the West Coast Brewery Tours bring in customers for both beer and spirits."

TOURS AND EVENTS

Moon Distillery is a stop on West Coast Brewery Tours' craft brewery and distillery tour. It also publicizes its products and cocktails on the usual social media sites and buys print ads in the local tourism guides.

Moon holds monthly Night School at the Brewery inter-active seminars, which include tastings of its products. The program covers topics such as "The History of Beer Making" and "The Brewing Process and Equipment." For another seminar, "All About Grain," Moon invited Kyle Mitchell, whose family has farmed on the Saanich Peninsula since 1862, and Mike Doehnel, a local master maltster. Kyle revealed his farm will be increasing barley and wheat crops, in part because craft distilleries are escalating demand for these grains.

The company also sponsors soccer, curling, and dragon boat teams. Most of the customers know the Moon name due to its longevity, craft beers, and, now, its participation in cocktail culture. The fact that people can dine, drink craft beer brewed on-site, and quaff cocktails mixed from spirits distilled on-site makes the company unique in the region.

Moon sells its products on-site, online, and in private liquor stores, as well as at various farmers' markets, the Nomad Holiday Market, and the Christmas Craft Fair on Salt Spring Island. It also participates in festivals such as Art of the Cocktail and Taste Victoria.

SIGNATURE COCKTAIL

THE MOON SHAFT

2 oz (60 mL) Shaft Liqueur

Splash of cream

Splash of honey

Mix and pour over ice.

4
PHILLIPS FERMENTORIUM DISTILLING COMPANY

MATT PHILLIPS, OWNER, BREWER, AND DISTILLER

2010 GOVERNMENT STREET

VICTORIA, BC V8T 4P1

250-380-1912

INFO@FERMENTORIUM.CA

FERMENTORIUM.CA

LATITUDE 48.432180, LONGITUDE -123.367520

DISTILLER MATT PHILLIPS STARTED HIS CAREER AS a brewmaster and has based many of his brewing and distilling talents on his degree in microbiology from Mount Allison University. "It's a great base," he says. "For example, it helps my knowledge of yeast. I know that when the yeast is happy, I'm happy." The Phillips company even became a partner in a University of Victoria experiment to develop a precise method of identifying when brewer's yeast has been exhausted and can no longer be reused.

The road to success for this entrepreneur was built on tenacity, risk taking, and the willingness to live without comfort—at least for a while. Wanting to perfect his knowledge of the art and science of beer brewing, he left the Atlantic for the Pacific: BC was *the* place for craft beer brewing. His first job was at Whistler Brewing; it offered a great training program. But the sea beckoned, and he moved to Victoria, taking a job at Spinnakers, Canada's oldest brew pub, founded in 1984.

By the mid-1990s, he'd gained much experience and wanted to develop his own brews. As he stated in a profile for *Business in Vancouver*, he'd put a few bucks aside, built a good credit rating, and written a business plan. He looked for additional financing. But the staid banks, as well as the risk-averse credit unions, thought his enterprise way too perilous and turned him down flat. Matt grabbed credit card applications on his way out the door and maxed them out to buy equipment. It was a heady period for craft brewers: many breweries were opening but not all were financially viable, allowing Matt to obtain some of his equipment at cut-rate prices.

By 2001, he'd unveiled his first 1,300-square-foot brewery in Esquimalt, on the second floor of an industrial building. Lacking cash flow, he bedded down (illegally) at the brewery for two years; fortunately, he could shower at a nearby gym. It was a completely do-it-yourself enterprise. He brewed the beer, bottled, labelled, packaged, and delivered it to various liquor stores in a rented U-Haul truck. His beers were bold and unorthodox, especially for the times: espresso stout, raspberry wheat ale, and a boldly hopped India pale ale.

He bought his glass bottles in Portland, Oregon, driving a large rented truck to the glass factory and loading up. One day, as he was meandering around the glass plant, he spotted stubbies—bottles that are shorter and flatter than standard beer bottles—tucked away in a corner. As his business wasn't growing very fast, and cash-flow problems plagued him, he'd almost given up on having his own craft brewery. What the heck, he said to himself, and decided to buy those stubbies and brew beer that would suit that bottle shape. The beer he put in those stubbies was named Phoenix Lager—rising from the ashes. Today Phillips brews 18 beers as part of its standard repertoire, as well as short runs of seasonal beers.

Phillips has built on the craft beer business, appealing to a younger group of imbibers who are interested in knowing where ingredients come from. They enjoy a multiplicity of locally made beers (and spirits) made with local ingredients—beers and liquors that have verve, with different, even wild, flavours.

MOVING TO GOVERNMENT STREET

In 2008, the company moved to much larger premises on Government Street, a semi-industrial zone north of the immediate downtown shopping area (there's much gentrification going on around the site today). Matt had obtained a distilling licence while still in Esquimalt.

But what motivated the move toward distilling was his desire to make tonic to pair with gin. "I got excited about gin," he says. "It was going to be a fun project. You know, making an old-fashioned G and T. But I got hung up on wanting to sell the tonic in cans, and no one I contacted would complete my small tonic runs. I didn't even think of bottling the tonic." Today, Phillips sells its two tonic flavours—Sparkmouth Artisanal Dry and Cucumber Mint—in cans. They contain half the sugar of non-artisanal tonics. The firm has also added a division called Phillips Soda Works to its repertoire: Spitfire Ginger Ale, Captain Electro's Intergalactic Root Beer, Speed King Craft Cola, and Dare Devil Orange Cream. I might be imagining it, but the names and label art are designed to fulfill the fantasies of young boys.

Matt chose the name Fermentorium for the distillery—a Phillips Distillery already existed in Minnesota. Along the way, he had obtained a huge old pot still. The still had been found in the Okanagan, where it once served in the Hiram Walker distillery. It was in pieces on pallets. Eventually, Rick Pipes of Merridale Cidery & Distillery (see chapter 8) bought it for the copper value but ended up selling the copper bits to Phillips. The still had been built in the UK, and no one knows for sure when it was constructed—I've been told a variety of dates, but most agree it's at least 90 years old. It's part of the copper still's mystery and mystique.

It was nicknamed Old George (although it was also known as Old Mama) and was moved in pieces to its new premises, where it languished. "We lacked the manpower to set up the old still," says Matt. Beer sales were so successful that distilling was put on the back burner. "It was after the government asked why we weren't using the still and threatened to revoke our licence that we went back to the idea of distilling. Specific Mechanical, the regional still fabricator, helped us put Old George back together."

To begin distilling, Phillips obtained the services of Master Distiller Laurent Lafuente. Laurent had first discovered Old George in the Okanagan and consults with many distilleries—both start-ups and mature ones. He started the processing of Phillips's gins and whiskies in 2014. "Laurent con-sulted with us and helped us in the early stages," says Matt. "It was

Laurent Lafuente with his whisky thief tasting a dram.

especially important for us to learn about the right cuts. The head cuts are pretty simple. You can smell the methanol. The maintenance team use it as a solvent in-house. It was the tails we had to know where to cut. We wanted to make clean cuts and produce a light-body ethanol. We redistill the tails with the heads, because it still contains a lot of alcohol. About 7 to 10 percent of tails go into the wash. The combination gives you an oilier mouth feel. But we are conservative in our cuts."

Laurent learned winemaking in Switzerland and subse-quently specialized in distilling. He's supplied his expertise to several start-up distilleries in BC. He also spent years oversee-ing research and development for a 50-million-litre rum dis-tillery in British Guiana. Of French origin, Laurent sees poetry in local distilling. "Making spirits is creative," he tells me. "What I want to reach is creativity in a bottle. When you drink craft spirits with friends, you know it's a special occasion. And when you buy a bottle of craft, you buy a piece of the soul of the people who created it. It brings little bits of happiness. Part of the spirit is the connection to the place we live. It's spiritual. We need roots. When we buy local, we're rooted. And Stump Gin is a true expression of the West."

Matt is highly pleased with having launched the distillery. "It's been a blast," he says. "The brewery is very busy, and that gives us patience to wait for spirit maturity. It's not a stretch to distill. It's fun, challenging, and a good add-on. We have the equipment that can cross over to some degree. We don't need to sell liquor for cash flow, so we can take our time."

That time is devoted to whisky. Phillips has some rye maturing and has launched three expressions of malt whisky with a maturity of five years or more. "By law we only have to store it for three years, but it wasn't where we wanted it to be after such a short time. We've given it five years, and it all seems to come together at that maturity."

The whiskies have been stored in casks previously containing bourbon, beer, or Pinot Noir. "We crank out 250 to 300 barrels a year," Matt continues. "Once mature, these whiskies are barrel blended. Blending is a whole separate art. For the gin, every batch is slightly different. We mature it in barrels too. It's an art, a fun art, for both the nose and the mouth."

The barley supplies the base for 18 types of beer brewed on-site and also for Fermentorium's signature Stump Coastal Forest Gin, promoted for its "bold flavours as undomesticated as the rugged BC coastline." Matt adds that to stay a true Vancouver Island gin, they had to avoid limes and lemons, as they don't grow here. "The hops and barley are a shout-out to who we are."

Phillips Maltworks, which supplies malted barley to many of Vancouver Island's distilleries.

The barley the Fermentorium uses is grown on the Saanich Peninsula and the rest of Vancouver Island. Phillips added its own malting plant in 2015. Colossal towers—two store barley, and the other two, malt barley—are located behind the brewing/ distilling building. Malting is the process when grains germinate or sprout in water. The wetted grain is then dried, and when put in a mash tun it produces the needed enzymes for brewing and distilling. "People don't often realize that barley must be malted before you can use it in making alcoholic beverages," Matt says. "We're now one of only three or four craft breweries/distilleries in North America with its own malting plant."

Phillips's distiller, Damon Bell, with Old George.

HEAD DISTILLER DAMON BELL

One of the people who worked—and trained—with Laurent Lafuente is Damon Bell, now Phillips's main distiller (he's nicknamed Deebs). "We added a made-in-Germany Müller Brennerei pot still in 2014," he tells me while standing by Old George. "The two stills are connected. The Müller still distills the gin and the Hop Drop liqueur that can be savoured neat or cannonballed into beer."

During my interview with him, a "low wine" run through Old George transfers to the Müller and enters its second distillation. Damon checks the computer on a stand near the Müller still. "We use in-house automation software," he says. "And we have techs on-site giving us the ability to instantly tweak such items as temperature and timing."

Damon, wearing a baseball cap and plaid shirt and sporting a trimmed black beard, hails from Manitoba. His father was a home brewer, and Damon learned at his dad's knee. He met Matt while working in an Esquimalt U-brew next door to Matt's start-up brewery. "I watched this one-man operation with him doing all the jobs. One day I helped him bottle his beer. He was brewing Phoenix, which kept the fires burning. We got to know each other, and that's how I became a brewer. I've been with Phillips for 17 years," Damon says.

"I remember the grain fields in my home province, and they're enormous. Here on Vancouver Island the barley comes from small fields, and we malt and distill smaller batches and put them in small bottles." He explains that the small, local grain fields have a fairly consistent yield. Although no one can control the weather, the region usually has good moisture for growing barley in the spring, followed by long, hot summers. The grain has time to ripen, unlike in Alberta, where a snowstorm can show up in late August and kill the crop.

"I learned distilling on the job," Damon says. "I got pointers from Laurent Lafuente. I badgered him for information. He's very European, very romantic about distilling, very hands-on. I learned to make the head cuts primarily by nose, the tails by flavour."

Damon also read "endless" treatises on the theory of distilling but believes that, for him, having a mentor, someone with great distilling experience, is much better than going to school in Scotland. "Becoming a sponge to a mentor, learning patience, and having faith have been my education."

He says that for a 200-litre batch, the first 2 litres are methanol and the tails run about 10–15 litres, leaving around 183–188 litres of heart. "These numbers are approximate and also depend on the strength of the wash."

The malting process takes about seven days: the barley steeps for two days, germinates for four, then dries for about one to one and a half days. After the barley has malted, it's put in a mash tun with hot water to extract the starch that creates the wort, which in turn is fermented. The fermented liquid, now called the wash, contains about 10 percent alcohol barley malt beer that is poured into Old George for its stripping run and then stored in an intermediate bulk container tote. The resulting low wine will have two possible destinations: To make whisky, the low wine is redistilled in Old George's copper innards to produce an intense and complex clear spirit, which will then spend at least three years in used oak barrels to gain colour, aroma, and flavours. The second method redistills the low wine through the Müller pot still's rectification column, where it becomes a neutral base with a purity of 95 percent alcohol before it is infused and redistilled with botanicals to make the two gins Phillips produces.

After distilling about 10 batches, or when changing to a different spirit, Damon cleans the stills with citric acid. "We need the copper to remove the sulphuric compounds created during distilling, but these can accumulate and distort the flavour," he tells me.

Phillips's spirits.

THE FERMENTORIUM'S SPIRITS

Stump Coastal Forest Gin is flavoured with locally foraged juniper, hops, bay laurel, coriander, lavender, fennel, and, to make the tang ever pinier, grand fir tips. According to Laurent, "drinking Stump is like walking through a coastal forest." The first run takes place in Old George, while the second distillation is performed in the Müller refractory still. Finally, the gin is redistilled with BC-grown botanicals. "We wanted Stump to be very distinctive, to be very Vancouver Island," says Damon. "The grand fir is foraged for us in the region by a First Nations specialist. He collects a couple of times a year and chooses mature branches with the firm flavour of mature leaves—not tips, with their low flavour." The alcohol by volume is 42 percent.

Discovery Gin is named after the cross street where Phillips is located. This gin is considered a "friend of cocktails." It contains the aromas of juniper, coriander, grains of paradise (a species in the ginger family), grapefruit and lemon peel, and cassia bark. The alcohol by volume is 43 percent.

Small Talk Whisky has had two releases, and more is maturing in casks. "It's based on the unique characteristics of Saanich Peninsula barley," says Damon. The whisky is blended from spirits that matured in casks previously containing bourbon, beer, or Pinot Noir. The alcohol by volume is 45 percent.

THE TASTING ROOM

Phillips has licences for a tasting room that serves 16 craft beers on tap, as well as its spirits. A space is also reserved for merchandise, including the tonics, the sodas, various canned beers, and the three spirits. Snacks include a cheeseboard,

Phillips's art deco sign.

meat sticks infused with Phillips's own craft beer, and giant fresh pretzels with homemade mustard. The tasting room's large indoor windows allow patrons to see the bottling area and get a glimpse of an active working brewery.

A record player, suitably placed on a cask, was blasting out 1960s rock on 33 rpm vinyl while I visited. An old-fashioned jukebox with "25 original records and stars" was stationed behind the barrel.

When I walked outside the tasting room, located on the corner of Government and Discovery Streets, I noted the art deco sign: Phillips Brewing Co. The blue and gold sign, with its neon tubes fixed on the outside, certainly resembles a vintage logo and provides the company with a sense of longevity. I asked Matt if he'd located this sign in some old shop or warehouse. "No," he responded. "The sign was specially made for the opening of the tasting room three years ago. We wanted something to fit the art deco style of the building."

As I was leaving Phillips, I saw a staff member with a broom and dustpan picking up cigarette butts in the parking lot where smokers had stomped on them the previous night. It's not just the inside of the brewery-distillery that is organized and tidy—it extends to the parking lot.

AWARDS

Stump Gin has won the following awards:
- Silver medal with distinction, 2019 Canadian Artisan Spirit Competition
- Bronze medal, 2018 Canadian Artisan Spirit Competition
- Silver medal, International Contemporary Grain-to-Glass Gin category, and bronze medal, Excellence in Packaging, American Distilling Institute 2017 Judging of Craft Spirits Awards

EVENTS

Phillips hosts a three-night music festival called the Phillips Backyard Weekender every summer. The parking lot opens and allows hordes of ticket buyers to enjoy music and beer. It's a 19-plus event.

Phillips's bar is very popular.

Phillips also sponsors Benefit Brew, an annual program in which the public nominates a favourite charity. The nominations are winnowed to 10, and the public again votes for the winner. The 2019 winner, for example, was Ocean Wise, a non-profit organization dedicated to protecting the health of our oceans. For each winner, Phillips develops a special beer and, working with the non-profit, a specially de-signed label. The full proceeds of the special beer sales are donated to the cause. Past winners include the Victoria Humane Society, the Dogwood Rescue Society, and the BC SPCA Wild Animal Rehabilitation Centre.

SIGNATURE COCKTAILS

STUMP AND TONIC

1 oz (30 mL) Stump Coastal Forest Gin

3 dashes Fee Brothers Grapefruit Bitters

One of Phillips's artisanal tonics

Grapefruit wedge

Build over ice in a wineglass and garnish with a grapefruit wedge.

WEST COAST GIMLET

1½ oz (45 mL) Stump Coastal Forest Gin

½ oz (15 mL) Hop Drop liqueur

½ oz (15 mL) sugar syrup (1:1 sugar and water)

¾ oz (22 mL) fresh lime juice

Lime wheel

Shake and double-strain into a large cocktail glass and garnish with a lime wheel.

5
SPINNAKERS

KALA HADFIELD, DISTILLER

308 CATHERINE STREET

VICTORIA, BC V9A 3S8

250-386-2739, TOLL-FREE 1-877-838-2739

SPINNAKERS@SPINNAKERS.COM

SPINNAKERS.COM

LATITUDE 48.429216, LONGITUDE -123.385045

KALA HADFIELD LAUNCHED HER NEW PRODUCTS—
Breakwater Vodka and Botanical Beach Gin—at the Art of the
Cocktail party in October 2019. But it certainly wasn't her
introduction to alcoholic beverages. In 1984, her father, Paul
Hadfield, founded the purpose-built Spinnakers Gastro Brewpub
when Kala was just learning to crawl. The building that houses
the pub and brewery, and now the distillery, incorporates large
windows providing excellent views of Victoria Harbour. It's a
popular gathering place.

Spinnakers was the first microbrew pub in Canada since
Canadian Prohibition, which lasted briefly from 1918 to 1920.
Since then, federal law had prohibited pubs and craft breweries from sharing the same premises. Hadfield and colleagues
had been petitioning federal and other government agencies to
change the law. Fortunately,
the change was enacted just
in time to make Spinnakers
a legal brew pub. In a 2017
interview with Joe Wiebe for
the *BC Ale Trail*, Paul Hadfield
told a story about how at one
point they thought they'd have
to put their beer in kegs, load
it on a truck, drive out of the
parking lot, turn around, come
back and load the kegs to the
serving area.

Spinnakers sign.

Kala recalls exploring the upstairs offices at the pub while
she was growing up, but being too young to enter the pub
where Spinnakers sold its on-site brewed craft beer and tasty
food. These offices have long been converted to serve the many

customers looking for a pint, a cocktail, and a full food menu based on locally grown fare.

All during her growing years Kala was exposed to the business of making beer and serving food. Many of the brewers and distillers in this book are family affairs, and some, like Spinnakers, are multigenerational. (Kala's sister, Carly Hadfield, and her partner, Troy Pyett, own the Lion's Head Smoke & Brew Pub in Castlegar, BC.)

When I met Kala, Spinnakers' tall distiller with long blond hair, she was a wearing a work uniform highlighting one of Spinnakers' beers—a T-shirt with a Jolly Hopper Imperial Pale Ale logo—and jeans. She served as one of Spinnakers' bartenders for a decade, dispensing beer in the taproom and mixing cocktails.

When one of the brewers left, Paul encouraged Kala to become involved in the brewery. She already knew she preferred production to working the front of the house. "In 2010, I started on the packaging line and making deliveries," she says. Over the next decade, she moved up through cellaring, brewing, and cider making to a management position. "I've been a 'brew-collar' worker," she quips.

To begin its distilling venture, Spinnakers purchased a still manufactured by iStill. As part of her distilling training, Kala signed up for a course with this still company, which was held in Napa Valley, California. "It was a week-long course, very hands-on," she says. "It included the theory of distilling too. But after the courses, you have to learn the actual process yourself. It's an intense experience." She adds that although presently she is the only distiller at Spinnakers, she is part of the team of brewers who provide the beer wash she uses as the base for distilling spirits.

THE STILL AND THE DISTILLING PROCESS

Spinnakers chose a Dutch-built still from iStill, a relative newcomer to distilling equipment fabrication. The stills it produces look different from traditional ones: they're square and insulated with black foam. The iStill website claims it is a 21st-century manufacturer and that its square-shaped stills are easier to fit into distilleries, with lower electrical demands and electronic systems that help craft distillers become more efficient. "iStill makes distilling easy," the company writes on its website. "The units come with various automated programs that help you mash, ferment, and distill. Also, all iStills can be connected to the internet. That way we can upload new firmware to your distillery multiple times per year."

Kala Hadfield by her iStill.

Kala notes that a "big deciding factor" in choosing the iStill was that it is powered by electricity—the Spinnakers brewery is also electric—and its "small footprint" fits well in the distillery's condensed space.

"With regard to the automated programs, they give a good starting point, but you still need to rely on your sense of smell and taste when making cuts, just like you would with more traditional stills," she says. "At this point we have not attempted any mashing or fermenting in the iStill.

"I already had a good background in making mashes and fermenting. The challenge lay in learning to use the equipment that gives rise to our smooth vodka. I did a lot of experimenting and redistilling. But the results are excellent. I'm distilling about 200 litres of finished product every month, and I will build on that to increase production. Of course, it takes vastly more volume passing through the still to produce just one litre of vodka or gin."

She has noted that in the brew pub, imbibers choose vodka twice as often as gin in their cocktail flights. But at private liquor stores, gin sales are more popular. "I must balance production to have enough of both spirits on hand," Kala says.

Her malted barley is delivered by Vancouver-based Country Malt. Earlier, at other distilleries, I'd seen malted-barley sacks weighing 2,000 kilograms. But at Spinnakers, the barley arrives in 25-kilogram sacks. I ask Kala why these bags are so small. She smiles and leads me up the stairs to the

The grist mill on Spinnakers' second floor.

second floor. In the far corner, a red-painted funnel/grinder drops the milled-on-the-spot malted barley two storeys down to the brewery/distillery directly into a mash tun. "It's the best location we have available for the funnel," says Kala. "And as we have to physically haul the barley up the stairs, 25 kilos is pretty much the limit."

She adds that production space is cramped, with beer and spirit fabrication sharing a ground-floor space. Spinnakers has thus been forced to place four stainless steel fermenting vats outside. Two additional plastic totes recapture and reuse the still's cooling water.

SPINNAKERS' PRODUCTS

After Kala imports Spinnakers' malted-barley craft beer wash into her still, she runs it four times to create the low wine she needs for one spirit run. She then distills it two more times for the Breakwater Classic Vodka and a third time to make the Botanical Beach Gins to reach at least 95 percent alcohol purity. When diluted, the vodka's alcohol by volume is 40 percent. Two versions of gin are on offer: a London dry type with an alcohol by volume of 43 percent and a Navy Strength style with a whopping 57 percent alcohol by volume.

To craft her gin, Kala adds nine botanicals in two stages. She first macerates juniper and coriander overnight, then adds grapefruit peel, bitter orange peel, angelica, hops, black pepper, cinnamon, and cardamom to create the gin's specific flavours.

Spinnakers' vodka.

Now that she has produced many batches of spirits, Kala is happy to have added distilling to her reservoir of talents. "It's fun," she says. "I love learning new skills. It's a challenge, and it's creative. I've been working on new flavours."

Thus, in early 2020, she launched a cassis liqueur flavoured with black currants, called Au Currant Crème de Cassis. Its alcohol by volume is 18 percent.

Chocoholic Crème de Cacao liqueur is made of vodka-infused cacao nibs and husks from Sirene Chocolate of Victoria and organic cane sugar syrup. Its alcohol by volume is 25 percent.

Cranberry Gin was next on the list of products. Kala laced her Botanical Beach Gin with Okanagan cranberry juice, organic cane sugar, and botanicals. Its alcohol by volume is 18 percent.

A different version of this tipple is Pink Grapefruit Gin, which, as its name implies, is flavoured with grapefruit, as well as other botanicals and organic cane sugar. Its alcohol by volume is 40 percent.

Kala has some sage advice for other women wishing to become distillers. "Just do it. Be prepared to start at the bottom, work hard, and get dirty."

When this book went into production, Spinnakers' spirit making was a recent venture. Therefore, it had not yet entered any spirit awards or become part of distillery tours (people do visit on the *BC Ale Trail*), or developed special cocktail recipes for its vodka and gin. I recommend that you check the website, spinnakers.com, to discover the latest spirits Kala has invented.

FAVOURITE COCKTAIL

CASSIS THE DAY

½ oz (15 mL) Spinnakers Breakwater Vodka

½ oz (15 mL) Spinnakers Au Currant Crème de
    Cassis

2 oz (60 mL) fresh lemon juice

Simple syrup to taste (1:1 sugar and water)

Top with Spinnakers O de Vie or other
sparkling water.

6
DEVINE
DISTILLERY
& WINERY

JOHN AND CATHERINE WINDSOR, OWNERS
KIRSTEN TITCOMB, GENERAL MANAGER
KEN WINCHESTER, MASTER DISTILLER
KEVIN TITCOMB, DISTILLER

6181B OLD WEST SAANICH ROAD

SAANICHTON, BC V8M 1W8

250-665-6983

INFO@DEVINEVINEYARDS.CA

DEVINEVINEYARDS.CA

LATITUDE 48.553535, LONGITUDE -123.430388

View from DEVINE across the fields toward Haro Strait
and Mount Baker.

IN 2007, JOHN AND CATHERINE WINDSOR SEARCHED
for a home on Vancouver Island, as their middle son, Ryan, had
moved there, and their daughter, Kirsten Titcomb, and her family
yearned to relocate to the Island. The Windsors didn't find a
house that suited them, but when a realtor showed them 23 acres
of fallow, overgrown farmland in Saanichton—a village in the
municipality of Central Saanich and the geographic heart of the
Saanich Peninsula—they were smitten.

It's clear why the property appealed. A curvy drive leads to
its high hill setting with outstanding vistas over the vineyard
and neighbouring farms. I visited on a bright, sunny autumn
day; farmhouses speckled the foreground, trees turned copper
and gold with masses of dark-green conifers interspersed among
them. Rows of espaliered vines, facing mostly south, crept down
the hillside. Looking east, beyond Haro Strait, layers of blue San

DEVINE's terrace.

Juan Islands seized the horizon while Mount Baker raised its glacier-capped head above them, flanked by the hazy outlines of other Cascade summits.

The tasting room is inviting, with a bar made from thick slabs of arbutus wood borne by wine barrels. The outside patio with its wrought-iron tables and chairs induces patrons to lounge, enjoy the outstanding views, and taste the wine and spirits along with some snacks.

I appreciate the company's tongue-in-cheek name, DEVINE. Their views are divine, their vines inhabit the property, and their products are divinely inspired.

"My dad was a real estate developer, and he saw value in the land," says Kirsten, DEVINE's chief financial officer and manager. "He made a real estate decision, although the property is in the Agricultural Land Reserve, with the requirement that agriculture be the primary use. With farm status, no one can subdivide the land. But my parents were able to build a house on the property.

"My mom was the romantic. 'It's so beautiful here,' she said. 'Let's grow grapes and make wine.' She had no idea how hard it is to grow grapes."

But the Windsors weren't deterred. With the public's growing interest in locally grown whole foods and the 100-mile diet, farm-to-glass wineries were sprouting in Vancouver Island's Cowichan Valley region and on the Saanich Peninsula. The region has 900–1,200 growing degree days, encouraging small-batch, handcrafted wineries to give it a shot. The Windsors took the plunge to establish a vineyard in 2008, under the guidance of winemaker and distiller Ken Winchester. They planted Pinot Gris and Pinot Noir grapes, as well as an Austrian white grape, Grüner Veltliner. They built the winery after the vines matured; the craft distillery was added in 2015. Some of the wines serve as the base for their distilled spirits.

Beginning a vineyard is labour intensive and time consuming. Property remediation was the first step for DEVINE. On south Vancouver Island, with its mild climate, plentiful winter rains, and warm, dry summers, the neglected vegetation had multiplied and invasive species had taken root. After the cleanup, the Windsors ensured the land and their vines could eventually be certified organic, avoiding sprays and pesticides from the beginning. They achieved that goal in February 2017 when they received certification. They also vowed that all of their products, wine and spirits, would be sustainably grown and harvested and that none would contain additives, preservatives, or artificial flavours. The company prides itself on its motto, "Good honest spirits made by hand and elegantly crafted from the heart."

Even all of its bottle labels are hand created by local artist Margaret Hanson, who uses linocuts to make the original images for each spirit brand. She also developed the DEVINE logo celebrating the grapevine that gave the winery its first successes.

A FAMILY BUSINESS

A Windsor has been running the business since DEVINE's beginning. For the first seven years, Ryan Windsor managed the winery, but he began stepping back from the company after being elected mayor of Central Saanich in 2014. The Windsor parents are mostly retired and spend at least half their time in Vancouver. Daughter Kirsten had been managing DEVINE's finances from Vancouver and realized that now was the time to hop west across the Strait of Georgia. She arrived on Vancouver Island with her husband, Kevin Titcomb, in 2017.

"It was a huge change for us," Kirsten tells me in DEVINE's tasting room. "Kevin had a career as an independent contractor, liaising between the owners and builders in development projects. It was an extremely high-pressure job, and after 20 or so years, he took a left turn and started learning to be a winemaker and distiller under the tutelage of our master distiller,

Distiller Kevin Titcomb explains about the grains in DEVINE's Ancient Grains whisky.

Ken Winchester. We love the Island. It's been a good decision to take that 180-degree turn."

Kevin has plunged into his new career. "Working at DEVINE is a totally different kind of stress from construction," he says. "A lot of new learning. Besides being educated by the hands-on work, I am taking a distance education program at the Institute of Brewing & Distilling in the UK."

He's thoroughly enjoying his new career. "Winemaking takes place once a year, but the distillery runs every day,"

Kirsten Titcomb in DEVINE's tasting room.

he says. "Most of the work is manual, really hands-on, but it's the art of producing our spirits I really enjoy. And I have a great partnership with our master distiller, Ken. He has so much experience and knowledge that I learn from. Working with him has been phenomenal."

He notes that much of what he learned in the construction business is applicable to a winery/distillery. "Ingredients, supplies, equipment, inventory, events, timing for a mash or a wash—they all need to be planned and coordinated."

Kirsten has completely immersed herself in running the business. DEVINE had been hosting weddings, but Kirsten found that increased local traffic interfered with the neighbours' peaceful weekends. "It was also incredibly labour intensive and took away from other duties. So we stopped hosting weddings and concentrated on the core business—making spirits and wine."

That concentration paid off. *Jim Murray's Whisky Bible 2018* listed DEVINE's Glen Saanich whisky at 94 points. Murray, a renowned whisky critic, terms whiskies between 94 and 97.5 points as "super whiskies." "When that ranking was published, Ken was speechless, floating through the day," says Kirsten. "For him, it was a dream fulfilled. Amazingly, the whisky was a new make, only one year old."

The DEVINE crew are planning an expansion of their brand and premises. "We are keeping the same tasting room," says Kirsten. "But we've maxed out the outdoor seating. We need more production and storage space and have plans for a second still."

Weather conditions also brought a change. In 2019, DEVINE ripped out three acres of vines. The area had become too wet and didn't produce the high-quality grapes required. To replace the vines, they planted the four ancient grains used in distilling their Ancient Grains whisky.

MASTER WINEMAKER AND DISTILLER KEN WINCHESTER

Ken came aboard as DEVINE's wine consultant in 2008 when the first vines were planted. He'd already launched Vancouver Island's first distillery the previous year. Ken has been one of the region's pioneers in producing and promoting small-batch, artisan spirits.

"I'm always looking for the next opportunity," he says. "That search has dominated my life." Born in Brooklyn, Ken attended Ohio's College of Wooster, located midway between Columbus and Cleveland. He then received a scholarship in environmental studies at the University of Toronto. Since then, he has bounced back and forth between the United States and Canada; his dual citizenship has aided him to pursue those new opportunities in both countries. "But," he says, "I've now spent more time in Canada than any place."

His earlier career—publishing—didn't necessarily link to making wine and distilled liquors. He served as editor and publisher at *Reader's Digest* and Time-Life Books, then founded Montreal book publisher St. Remy Press. Time Warner in New York City was next, and then a stint as editorial director at Sunset Books brought him to San Francisco. "Although I loved working in publishing," Ken says, "I also developed a parallel interest in wine and did some amateur winemaking in my garage."

That avocation led to his enrolment at the University of California, Davis's Wine Executive Program, "From Grape to Table." It's a well-known course offered by the university's Graduate School of Management and Department of Viticulture and Enology.

"I took the leap," he recalls, "and bought land in Paso Robles, then a backwater but now home to more than 200 wineries. It's about halfway between San Francisco and Los Angeles. The Paso Robles region is a hot place and well suited to growing Rhône varietals like Syrah, Grenache, and Mourvèdre. Winchester Vineyards was a successful venture, but after a while, I grew homesick for Canada."

He sold his winery and, with his family, arrived on Vancouver Island in 2002, a time he describes as "the frontier in winemaking and distilling." He leased a vineyard and bought additional grapes from other wineries, launching Winchester Cellars. He made Pinot Noir, which, he says, is a very fussy grape. He also consulted for other wineries and became the first winemaker at Church & State, whose vineyards occupy land a stone's throw from DEVINE. "I always take what nature gives me and try not to screw it up," he says, chuckling.

"I was successful but, as always, looking for the next opportunity. Craft wine was growing but the competition was fierce. Craft distilling, especially in the US, was becoming the next big thing. People began wanting more than a few limited brands producing tens of thousands of generic, homogenized spirits every day. Canada was virgin territory."

He'd already been experimenting with a small still in his basement, making grappa. Combining that avocation with his experience in wine fermentation, he decided to hone his skills by enrolling in the Michigan State University Artisan Distilling Program. "It was the only legal distilling program at the time," he says. "An intense, hands-on course with sophisticated test equipment."

He also attended the week-long Bruichladdich Malt Academy on the Isle of Islay in the Scottish Hebrides. Afterwards, like Graeme Macaloney at nearby Macaloney's Caledonian Distillery, he stayed on at the Bruichladdich Distillery (it means "stony beach"). "I spent three weeks under the tutelage of Jim McEwan, one of the best-known and most medalled whisky makers in the world," he says. Three more weeks visiting distilleries in Scotland, and picking up bits of know-how at each of them, rounded out his education. In 2007, Ken, with an investor/partner, started Winchester Spirits, which, along with Merridale Cidery & Distillery, became the first artisan distillery on Vancouver Island.

Creating a distillery at that time was daunting. British Columbia hadn't yet revised its regulations allowing craft and artisan distillers to set up shop. That meant that small-batch distillers were obliged to follow the same regulations as giant corporations like Seagram's. These rules rarely fit craft enterprises. Dealing with the BC Liquor Distribution Branch was irksome. Ken persisted, however, and the company's first release was Victoria Gin, marketed as "Canada's first premium gin." It galloped to success. "We made gin the first product," he says, "because you can make it relatively quickly and create cash flow. But once we nailed the recipe, I was keen to move on to other spirits."

Today, this early distillery is owned by Grant Rogers of the Marker Group and is continuing to make a multitude of spirits on the Sidney waterfront under the name Victoria Distillers (see chapter 7).

Ken joined DEVINE as winemaker. When he heard through the grapevine that craft distilling was about to become legal in British Columbia, and that government liquor store fees would no longer gobble up about $30 per bottle, he proposed adding a distillery to the premises. In addition, he argued, grape growing and winemaking are seasonal; thus a year-round distilling operation during fallow times made sense. And he had the experience of creating a distillery in the past. The Windsors agreed.

The first task was finding distilling equipment. "I went looking for used stills and stumbled upon one," says Ken. "It was a vintage Kothe still made in Eislingen by one of Germany's venerable family still makers. It was built to make schnapps from local fruit."

The still had become peripatetic, moving from Germany to a cider distillery in Nova Scotia, then crossing Canada to the Holman Lang Wineries Group in the Okanagan. Holman Lang went into receivership in 2010, and the still was purchased as part of a bankruptcy sale, winding up in pieces in a barn in Cowichan. "I bought it sight unseen from my friend Rick Pipes at Merridale Cidery & Distillery based on the fact that it was an outstanding German brand," says Ken.

Distillers Ken Winchester and Kevin Titcomb with Brünhilde.

It took almost a year to put her back together again. The pot, column, and condenser were in perfect shape, but much of the plumbing and wiring had to be replaced. He also changed the heating system from oil to propane and added several safety features to comply with modern standards. Once on-site, the still had to be properly installed, with suitable venting through the distillery room's roof, and complying with building, gas, and fire codes.

Ken is pleased with the still's attributes and performance. The pot is solid copper, but the external cover is fabricated from stainless steel and insulated to minimize heat loss and to lower energy demand. "Copper does three things," he explains. "It's acid resistant. It transfers heat readily. But most importantly it reacts with sulphur to help purify the spirit. Technically it's a column still, but I also refer to it as a pot still or single-batch still."

For the past five years, Ken has been playing Siegfried to Brünhilde, as the crew has nicknamed the still. "Craft distilled products make up only about 2 percent of sales in Canada," he says. "Lots of opportunity for growth."

Ken is also fascinated by the history of alcoholic drinks. He combs through older and traditional recipes from different countries and adapts them to DEVINE's terroir. He relishes the "creative freedom" that he's been able to cultivate.

Always searching for that next special flavour, he experiments and distills a variety of beverages. "We don't just use a formula or recipe," he says. "So every mash and every run is different. We're constantly tasting, not just watching dials. The big guys make the same product over and over. Their job is to make a consistent product. We don't believe in that here. We're okay with differences."

Although the distillery repeats a number of its spirits each year, small batches of specialty hooch are often introduced. In 2015, Ken took advantage of a bumper crop of wild blackberries to make wine. "I wasn't crazy about the result," he says, "so I distilled it and made it into a blackberry brandy, a bit like schnapps. It was excellent." DEVINE has some fruit trees on the property, which has resulted in small runs of Poire (pear), a brandy resembling Poire Williams, and Pomme (with five types of organic apples), a local version of Calvados.

When Ken and Kevin dream up a new drink, they make a trial batch of 50 litres and scale it up if it turns out well. "Still, there's always a question if it'll work," he says. "I like Jerusalem artichokes, so I tried to distill and flavour a batch with that root vegetable. It smelled terrible and it tasted disgusting. We dumped it."

DEVINE has avoided making vodka. "Everyone makes vodka, but I made it only once," says Ken. "It was for a special fundraiser, and we picked new Sitka tips and flavoured the vodka with them. But vodka isn't part of our standard products."

"There are four secrets to building a successful distillery," concludes Ken. "Quality, packaging, price, and story. Our story includes these important terms: local, unique, and handmade. People drop by and ask, 'What's new?' DEVINE will continue to build on that story, and on our quality and innovation."

A sculpture representing the "angel's share."

DEVINE'S SPIRITS

Ken calls Glen Saanich single malt whisky his "baby." Its tag line is "A good honest whisky made by hand." Saanich Peninsula–grown malted barley provides the base ingredient for this handmade whisky. It's distilled twice and aged for at least three years in once-used bourbon casks. Not all of Glen Saanich has been released; part of it continues to age and is often tested for its evolving taste. The alcohol by volume is 45 percent. *Jim Murray's Whisky Bible 2020* score: 88.

Ancient Grains is "an authentic BC alternative young whisky," one that breaks the rules and traditions of whisky making. Although this "alt whisky" still uses malted barley as part of its base, it also includes Ken's predilection for unorthodox local and terroir flavours. He's chosen to add four other grown-in-BC grains to the mix—spelt, emmer, Khorasan wheat, and einkorn. They are the ancestors or cousins of modern wheat. Once distilled, the unique flavour fusion is aged in new, American oak quarter casks. These casks have a significantly higher ratio of wood to liquid than standard casks, which tends to accelerate the maturation process. The alcohol by volume is 45 percent. *Jim Murray's Whisky Bible 2020* score: 91.5.

DEVINE makes four kinds of gin, each with its own pedigree. Ken calls them "the history of gin in four bottles." Genever is the great-great-great-grandmother of all gins. Originally crafted in the Netherlands in the early 1600s, when Dutch galleons scoured the world to find—and monopolize—spices, this gin has spawned all the gins that have been made since. Ken starts with malted barley as the base, then adds 20 botanicals, including some unfamiliar ones: mugwort, wormwood, horehound, and blessed thistle. To reinforce the roots of this original Dutch-style genever recipe, the bottle label depicts the fictional story of the boy who stuck his finger in the dike and saved the city of Haarlem. The alcohol by volume is 45 percent.

Dutch Courage is a spirit unique to DEVINE—its tag line is "Old World gin meets New World whisky." It takes Genever and matures it in casks that formerly stored Ancient Grains alternative whisky. The barrels in which spirits are matured can be an important part of a distiller's tool kit. Choices include size, new or used oak, the origin of the oak, whether it's been charred or recharred, and what spirit or spirits were housed in it before. Dutch Courage, by being stored in previously housed Ancient Grains casks, amalgamates the essence and aroma of the five grains along with wormwood, mugwort, and juniper. The alcohol by volume is 45 percent.

A few centuries after it was invented, Ken has reimagined Vin Gin, a modern-day classic style of gin, which DEVINE describes as "London dry meets Pacific Northwest." Ten botanicals flavour this gin, including juniper, coriander, orange peel, lavender, and young spruce tips. In addition, Vin Gin is unusual in that it uses DEVINE's estate-grown Pinot Gris and Grüner Veltliner as well as other Vancouver Island wine grapes as the base. The alcohol by volume is 45 percent.

DEVINE transforms its Vin Gin into a second-generation New Tom barrel-aged gin and, through its maturing process, honours this mostly forgotten gin style. Rather than bottling the gin immediately after it's distilled, this gin is aged for up to three months in once-used bourbon casks, transmuting it with a bourbon piquancy and tinting it golden. The alcohol by volume is 45 percent.

The ancestor of this gin, known as Old Tom, was a mainstay in 18th-century London. As Wikipedia explains it, some publicans used the symbol of the black cat (the old tom) to signal to passersby that gin could be imbibed without entering. Once the customer dropped a coin in the cat's mouth, a shot of gin would pour through a tube into the parched mouth on the street. DEVINE has further resurrected the gin's tradition by portraying a black cat on the bottle label.

A sample of DEVINE's products.

To make its Sloe Gin, DEVINE added wild sloe berries (a tiny member of the plum family) to its classic gin and "brought an old English tradition to Canada," explains Ken. "So far, we're the only ones making it in British Columbia. Sloe berries aren't native to Canada—they were brought here from the UK about a century ago." Sloe berries often grow in hedgerows, look a bit like blueberries, and are painful to pick, as their branches are covered with savage spines. But Ken believes the tart flavour and ruby tint they add to the gin is worth the sting of collecting the berries. DEVINE made 700 litres in 2019. "It's a full-strength gin without added sugar," says Ken. The alcohol by volume is 45 percent.

Ken loves rum. To make Honey Shine Amber, with its tag line "Pure honey goodness, distilled," DEVINE has substituted honey for the traditional molasses, as sugar cane doesn't grow in BC. Two vast vats hold 4,000 litres of fermenting honey, which takes five weeks to be ready for distilling—much longer than any other DEVINE base fermentation. After the honey is fermented and distilled, it's aged on-site in once-used bourbon casks, which give it its caramel colour. The alcohol by volume is 42 percent.

Honey Shine Silver Beekeeper's Reserve, with its tag line "Where Vancouver Island meets Barbados," uses fermented, wild-gathered clover honey and turns it into a dry mead, which is then double-distilled in the style of a Caribbean rum. The alcohol by volume is 42 percent.

Black Bear Spiced Honey Rum, described as "dark and spicy like a true pirate's rum," started as a seasonal spirit but is now a staple. Its unique flavour is derived from the addition of cinnamon, vanilla, nutmeg, black pepper, allspice, and star anise during its maturation time. The alcohol by volume is 42 percent.

DEVINE also makes two fortified wines. Bianca Vermouth, which DEVINE calls "a classic James Bond martini ingredient," is crafted from Island-grown white wine grapes and fortified by house-distilled honey spirit. This vermouth can be quaffed on its own, paired with tonic or soda, and incorporated in martinis or other cocktails.

Moderna Vermouth, as its name implies, is a modern take on the original Turin recipe. "It's an authentic re-creation of an 18th-century northern Italy, Turin recipe," Ken says. This fortified wine combines Vancouver Island white wine with honey spirit and is scented with more than 30 different botanicals, including dried orange, clove, cardamom, rose, and juniper, and such more obscure flavourings as wormwood, sarsaparilla, and dittany of Crete. Alcohol by volume for both vermouths is 18 percent.

Vermouth can serve as a useful aperitif and has been touted as a digestive for hundreds of years.

AWARDS

The distillery has won an abundance of awards since 2016 for just about all its products. "The Canadian Whisky Awards are important," Ken says. "They allow us to show our spirits alongside some venerable producers from both Canada and the world."

For Glen Saanich single malt whisky, the most important awards have been a gold medal with distinction and best in class at the 2019 Canadian Artisan Spirit Competition, and a ranking of 94 in *Jim Murray's Whisky Bible 2018*.

Ancient Grains alt whisky secured a Best Whisky Spirit gold medal at the 2020 Canadian Whisky Awards, as well as a gold medal with distinction at the 2019 Canadian Artisan Spirit Competition. *Jim Murray's Whisky Bible 2019* scored it at 91.5 points.

Genever's most prestigious win was at the 2019 San Francisco World Spirits Competition with a best-in-class double gold award. Honey Shine Amber obtained gold at the Canadian Artisan Spirit Competition in 2018 and gold with distinction in 2019.

TASTING ROOM, TOURS, AND EDUCATION

DEVINE's tasting room is open to the public. To check both its seasonal schedule and special events, visit devinevineyards.ca.

Master Distiller Ken Winchester teaches a seminar on whisky making, demonstrating Brünhilde's functions, choosing grains, selecting barrel types, and aging styles. Check the schedule of upcoming seminars on the website.

SIGNATURE COCKTAIL

DEVINE INTERVENTION

1½ oz (45 mL) Genever
½ oz (15 mL) Moderna Vermouth
Lemon twist

Build in a glass over ice with tonic. Garnish with a lemon twist.

7
VICTORIA DISTILLERS

PETER HUNT, PRESIDENT AND MASTER DISTILLER

9891 SEAPORT PLACE

SIDNEY, BC V8L 4X3

250-544-8217

HELLO@VICTORIADISTILLERS.COM

VICTORIADISTILLERS.COM

LATITUDE 48.650264, LONGITUDE -123.394187

FEW COMPANIES HAVE THE LOCATION AND VIEW
Victoria Distillers enjoys. Sited between the Sidney Pier Hotel and
the Port Sidney Marina, the facility lies on Haro Strait with a first-
class vista of the Gulf and San Juan Islands.

The stylish wood and corrugated metal building on Seaport
Place might be considered a 21st-century version of the "gin
palaces" so popular in Britain in the 1800s. Except that Victoria
Distillers, with its 8,500-square-foot cocktail lounge, tasting
room, and distilling areas, does not bear any of the vulgar taints
attributed to the baroque bars of the past. About the only aspect
it has in common with these former drinking establishments is
the large windows that provide a terrific view of glacier-clad
Mount Baker standing proud behind San Juan Island. Instead of
mirrors, carved wood, and gilded mouldings, the facility has an
open feel with comfortable seating inside and on the patio.

While visiting the tasting room, I watched sailboats and
powerboats glide to and from the Port Sidney Marina and
observed the antics of owners and their dogs walking the
charming seaside boulevard, which doubles as the town's
sculpture walk.

Grant Rogers, whose Marker Group owns Victoria Distillers'
premises, told me he'd bought the property as part of Sidney's
revitalization program. Grant is a hometown guy, born and
raised in Sidney, and his company is described by the *Peninsula
News Review* as having "literally changed the face of Sidney
over the years." The Marker Group built the Sidney Pier Hotel
and neighbouring residences as well as a number of apartment/
condo buildings and townhouses.

Before the distillery occupied its present site, the building
was turning into a white elephant. "Although the location is
prime, I had difficulties leasing it," Grant says. "It was sad to

Victoria Distillers in Sidney.

have it sit empty. In the past, it had been a restaurant, and it also served for a while as a set for the television show *Gracepoint*. A brewery approached me but asked me to fund them so they could operate. That wasn't part of our business plan."

Perhaps some "spirit" intervened. In 2015 Grant took the risk to buy Victoria Spirits, then located on West Saanich Road, from Bryan and Valerie Murray. "It was a lucky accident," says Grant. "Creating premium alcoholic beverages certainly wasn't in our development portfolio. But the distillery has turned out to be a success, a terrific addition to the waterfront and Sidney's renaissance. It's a destination now. It makes products becoming appreciated internationally. And it's fun."

As part of the Marker Group, the company was rebranded and renamed Victoria Distillers. It took nearly a year to renovate the formerly vacant building. Fortunately, its roofs were high enough to accommodate the tall stills and their extensive plumbing. Through the building's main door, one enters the cocktail lounge with groups of tables and chairs in front of the bar. In the summer, the lounge extends onto a patio shielded from the sun by colourful umbrellas. Banks of bright yellow black-eyed Susans flank the perimeter.

Behind the bar, Kenzie Rutherford whips up a smoky cocktail. With a propane torch, she targets a small chunk of charred oak placed on a wooden board, then traps the smoke in an upside-down glass and combines it with Oaken Gin, maple syrup, Bittered Sling's Kensington Bitters and Moondog Bitters. The glass transmits the smoky flavour that complements the cocktail, and voila—the Oak Fashioned Cocktail. The mixologist can also launch individual and flights of other cocktails.

Kenzie Rutherford chars oak to make a smoky cocktail.

Beyond the cocktail lounge and bar lies the spacious tasting room that overlooks the ocean and hosts small tours and larger events. A cask supports a tiny copper still that actually works. Bottles containing the botanicals that flavour the gins are arranged on the table. The original 200-litre Müller pot still is visible behind glass. "For the first 10 years, we used the Müller for all our production," says Peter Hunt, Victoria Distillers' president and master distiller. "Originally, it was wood fired. Now we employ it for small-batch spirits, rum, vodkas, and so on. And we also use it for R and D."

Peter Hunt with one of the company's stills.

INSIDE THE DISTILLERY

Two 900-litre stills were craned into place to join the older Müller pot still. They were both built by Specific Mechanical Systems, a local company manufacturing distillery and brewery equipment. "We're pleased to have found a local manufacturer that specializes in distillery equipment," says Peter. "We didn't have to go to Europe to import stills. The company customized the stills for us. They're versatile because they can convert from column still to pot still by replacing stainless columns with copper segments and hoods. Old stills may have history and patina, but modern stills include instrumentation that monitors temperature, although the process continues to be handcrafted."

The distillery's renovation also included some green initiatives. As the Marker Group owns the Sidney Pier Hotel next door, the distillery was able to integrate its plumbing systems with the hotel's HVAC system. The hotel had already installed such efficient systems as geothermal heat pumps that warm and cool the building by borrowing and returning excess heat from the ocean. The heat pumps reduce electricity consumption by as much as 60 percent. At the distillery, boilers heat the ethanol to its boiling point of 78.4°C (173.1°F), which separates it from most of the water it contains. Rather than being poured down the drain, that hot water runs through a heat exchanger. The energy is sent next door into the hotel and heats the rooms eight months a year, saving more than 800,000 kilojoules of heat and 4,000 litres of water from every distillation.

The renovated space allowed for the exploration of different projects. Distiller Leon Webb joined the team and made rum and whisky (he's now distilling at Shelter Point Distillery in Campbell River; see chapter 21). Today, Phil Lecours is the

Inside Victoria Distillers.

company's head distiller and is aided by Dave Clark. Peter, Phil, and Dave distill all the company's beverages.

"In 2009, we began collaborating with Phillips Brewing," says Peter. "Phillips prepared our barley wash, as we don't own large fermenting vats. After distilling the product, we matured it in new American quarter casks and other casks that had earlier stored bourbon. We released our Craigdarroch Whisky in 2015. It has sold out."

Victoria Distillers doesn't fit into British Columbia's definition of craft, which stipulates that the main ingredients be grown in the province. For its gin and vodka, Victoria Distillers orders its 100 percent, non–genetically modified, corn-based ethanol, which has already been distilled once, from Ontario. The ethanol arrives in square, 1,000-litre plastic totes. Victoria Distillers fits the definition of artisan distillery, where handcrafted, small

batches of spirits are made on-site. Although its gins are now selling internationally, the quantities remain limited in comparison with the megafactory producers like Gordon's or Tanqueray. Victoria Distillers also makes rum from imported molasses and organic fairtrade cane sugar. This isn't possible under the restrictive craft licence.

Bartender Cam Watson. Courtesy Victoria Distillers.

The botanicals that flavour the gin are sourced from around the world, which, Peter says, gives the distillery the widest possible opportunity to choose the best ingredients and create world-class products.

THE EVOLUTION OF VICTORIA DISTILLERS

Bryan Murray, the former owner of Victoria Spirits, had been an investor in Ken Winchester's winery (Ken is now master distiller and winemaker at DEVINE Distillery & Winery; see chapter 6). The team bought one of the venerable German-made Müller pot stills in 2007 to make wine-based brandies; the still remains part of the company's equipment.

Peter Hunt represents the next generation. He's Bryan Murray's stepson and started working with Victoria Spirits from its early beginnings. "I worked and trained with Ken," says Peter.

"Months after we opened, in 2008, we launched our premium Victoria Gin at the former Bengal Lounge at the Empress Hotel. Victoria Gin became our primary product for nearly a decade. It became the second-best premium gin seller in Canada after Hendrick's. [Hendrick's makes its gins in Scotland.] Today, our second gin, Empress 1908 Gin, outsells every gin in the category."

Peter joined the distillery full-time after putting his master's degree in molecular biology and genetics to work at the BC Cancer Agency. "I had a job as a genomics technologist in Vancouver, but I distilled on the weekends in Victoria," he says. "My science degrees also helped me in the art and science of distilling. I gained great practical experience. Very hands-on. And as I'd already worked as a bartender and bar manager at Victoria's Swans Brewery and Pub for a decade, I'd learned lots about liquor and cocktails. I began distilling with Ken, but after he left, I started distilling according to my own lights."

He's also worked as a volunteer in international development in Uganda, participating in studies to determine if soil-based selenium could help delay the onset of AIDS in HIV-positive people. While there, he met his wife, Natalie. Peter would like to go back to volunteering in Uganda, but at the moment, the couple's two young children prevent long periods away from home.

Peter works with distiller Phil Lecours, who hails from Montreal. Before his distilling career, Phil pursued a 20-year career as a chef and developed a fantastic palate—a huge asset to the team. All his distilling talents have been refined on the job; he's been at Victoria Distillers for more than a decade. He enjoys a nice glass of red but also likes a Victoria Gin and tonic with a lot of citrus.

Dave Clark rounds out the distilling team. He grew up in Lethbridge, Alberta, and spent time moving ever farther west with stopovers in the Kootenays, the Okanagan, Vancouver, and Whistler. He studied at Thompson Rivers University and worked in tourism and hospitality. He spent more than a decade as a bartender and mixologist and earned a brewing/distilling diploma after joining Victoria Distillers six years ago. He remarks that since he became involved in the spirits craft, "the industry has changed dramatically. Consumers are curious and love to imbibe new creative cocktails by trusted mixologists."

THE TWO FLAGSHIP GINS

With Victoria Gin, the company carved out a niche—it was the first premium small-batch gin made in Canada. "We've always been and continue to be a gin company," says Peter. Victoria Gin grew fairly rapidly in the first years, although the margins were small. Ten botanicals flavour the spirit, including juniper, coriander, cinnamon, lemon peel, orange peel, rose petal, angelica root, sarsaparilla, star anise, and orrisroot. The botanicals are all soaked overnight in the ethanol and then distilled, creating a balanced gin that mixes well with a wide variety of cocktails. (Many recipes are listed at victoriagin.com.) Compared with an average London dry gin, Victoria Gin's juniper flavouring is milder, less resiny. Peter says that juniper species number more than 50, and their berries differ in flavour. "For our gins, we import juniper berries from Macedonia. It's one of the world's prime juniper producers, and we chose their blue-tinted aromatic berries because their flavour is less powerful." Victoria Gin's alcohol by volume is 42.5 percent.

Empress 1908, one of Victoria Distillers' flagship gins.

Victoria Distillers' second flagship gin, Empress 1908, launched in 2017 and is keeping the company extremely busy. (The 1908 refers to the year Victoria's Empress Hotel was built.) Peter had reached out to the Empress, one of the grandes dames of the old Canadian Pacific Railway hotel networks. He asked the food and beverage group if they'd be interested in a collaboration. "They were excited by the idea," says Peter, "and we decided to draw on the Empress's famous afternoon tea for inspiration."

Empress 1908's website (empressgin.com) describes the Empress's afternoon tea, often called high tea, as "the curation of an exclusive collection of seasonal, hand-picked tea leaves, blended to create the perfect cup." Peter wanted to create a traditional gin with a modern twist, which he believes mirrors the Empress itself—an iconic, more than a century-old hotel with modern decor and comfort.

The botanicals flavouring Empress 1908 Gin.

The gin uses the same non–genetically modified corn ethanol as the base. Its botanicals include Macedonian juniper berries, grapefruit peel, coriander seed, rosebuds/petals, ginger root, and cinnamon bark. These six botanicals go into the pot, macerate overnight, and are then distilled with the ethanol.

The next step distinguishes this gin from the vast majority of other gins. The distillery infuses the distillate with the Empress's signature tea blend along with a botanical called the butterfly pea blossom, also called blue tea, a caffeine-free herbal tea grown in Southeast Asia. It's the butterfly pea blossom that gives Empress 1908 its unusual indigo colour.

"We always start our distillation process with our 96 percent ethanol, which has already been distilled once," Peter explains. "The spirit then rests for a month in a 9,000-litre tank. The final product is a modern version of traditional London dry gin, but with a unique character and that intriguing indigo hue. When mixed with ingredients like citrus or tonic, the blue colour changes to pink or violet. Add cucumber and the colour will turn turquoise or blue."

Empress 1908 has seen explosive growth: it is now the third-best-selling gin in BC. It's sold in at least seven countries, including New Zealand, Japan, the UK, and Switzerland. It's also distributed in seven provinces and most US states. It has become Victoria Distillers' best-selling product and has its own website, empressgin.com. Its slogan: "Live colourfully."

When I visited, the bottling station was fully stocked with Empress 1908 bottles. As they were filled and corked on the as-sembly line, a worker ran the bottles through the labelling machine, then loaded them into six-bottle boxes. As I left the distillery, a large truck was being loaded exclusive-ly with Empress 1908.

THE MARKETING

Victoria Distillers has fully embraced social media as marketing tools. Three

A sea of Empress 1908 Gin bottles.

websites highlight the company: victoriadistillers.com, victoriagin.com, and empressgin.com. Want to learn about "shaken, not stirred"? A Victoria Distillers bartender explains on victoriagin.com. There's a bit of print marketing that's still of use, and there are tastings in liquor stores. Sometimes, the sales team goes to bars and restaurants with samples, with the goal to appear on the menu.

Tours bring in many locals and tourists. Tastings can be accompanied by charcuterie boards, veggies, hummus, and nuts. The company partners with different organizations for events like wine festivals or charity fundraisers. Bottles are donated to auction fundraisers away from the distillery.

But for getting the biggest marketing bang for the buck, the internet rules. Under the guidance of marketing manager Jessalyn Pechie, the company's Twitter, Facebook, Pinterest, and Instagram accounts offer numerous cocktail recipes, which push audiences toward the websites and, it is hoped, to liquor stores. When people comment online, Jessalyn often responds. Using Victoria Distillers' gins as the main ingredient, YouTube tutorials show how to shake, garnish, pour, and muddle a cocktail. Even the right way to crush ice is shown.

"For our Empress 1908 Gin, we target the 25-to-40 age group, the urban millennials who seek experiences," says Jessalyn. "They're interested in sustainability and local products that differ from homogenous corporate ones. We emphasize the premium quality of our gins and target the more experienced cocktail crowd."

The goal is to foster community engagement and build relationships. Victoria Distillers sends samples to fashionable bartenders and mixologists with big followings in cities like Los Angeles and New York. These semi-celebrity social media influencers comment online or post a beautiful photo of a cocktail made with the two gins, encouraging consumers to order them and find outlets where the gins are sold.

Victoria Distillers marries social media and personal contact by inviting influencers, some of whom work in popular bars. During the summer, they fly four groups of four or five influencers to Victoria, lodge them at the Empress Hotel, and host them at the distillery. They go on bike tours, watch whales, and sample the culinary locations that serve Empress 1908 Gin and local, organic fare.

"It's the way to build relationships. These visits show the people behind the gin. It's much more than bottles on a shelf," explains Jessalyn.

"Thousands of people respond," she says. "And Empress 1908's indigo colour, with its changes to pink and lavender, are of great value. It shows well on Instagram photos."

VICTORIA DISTILLERS' OTHER PRODUCTS

Victoria Distillers' vodka is made in small batches with 100 percent non–genetically modified corn as the base. It is first distilled in Austria. This neutral spirit is clean with a crisp finish and suits flavoured cocktails. Alcohol by volume is 40 percent. It's only sold in the tasting room and used in cocktails on-site.

Left Coast Hemp Vodka is distilled with organic Canadian hemp seeds and creates a mixture of grassy/green and toasted nutty flavours. The base is the same non–genetically modified corn ethanol used in all Victoria Distillers' spirits. The oils from the hemp seed generate a rich texture that infiltrates the alcohol. It mixes well with coffee or chocolate, in a Caesar or Bloody Mary, or on its own in a martini. Alcohol by volume is 42 percent. It's only sold in the tasting room and used in cocktails on-site.

Smooth and buttery, Oaken Gin matures in new American oak casks, creating vanilla and caramel impressions. Alcohol by volume is 42.5 percent. It's only sold in the tasting room and used in cocktails on-site.

Sidney Spiced is a classic rum, made with molasses and organic, fair-trade cane sugar. It is spiced with vanilla, orange, ginger, star anise, and orrisroot. Alcohol by volume is 42.5 percent. It's only sold in the tasting room and used in cocktails on-site.

Aged for a total of five and a half years in a combination of American and French oak barrels, Victoria Distillers' brandy is a warm classic perfect for sipping beside the fire. It has oak overtones and can be tasted only in the Victoria Distillers tasting room.

Victoria Distillers teamed with Victoria-based Sirene Chocolate to create Chocolate Liqueur, which can be quaffed on its own, added to cocktails or coffee, or poured over ice cream. The spirit is made from fair-trade cane sugar, fair-trade cacao nibs (small pieces of crushed cacao beans), and cacao husks (the fibrous outer shells of the cacao bean). The cacao nibs and husks are infused after the ethanol is distilled. The cacao is supplied by Costa Esmeraldas in Ecuador. Alcohol by volume is 18 percent.

In early 2020, Victoria Distillers diversified by launching a new line of ready-to-drink beverages, the Strait & Narrow Pacific Coast Cocktails. Using its own handcrafted gins and a variety of botanicals, the distillery makes gin cocktails available in 355-millilitre cans in three flavours: grapefruit rosemary, lemon lavender, and pear rhubarb. The alcohol by volume is 5 percent.

During the COVID-19 pandemic, Peter Hunt quickly petitioned the BC government to add a product: hand sanitizer. "We started using the heads from our gin distillation process," Peter tells me. "We were producing 40 litres a day. It wasn't enough. So we teamed up with Nezza Naturals, a local company making organic body products." The distillery then used its 95 percent ethanol and blended it with vegetable glycerine and sweet orange essential oil. The product was distributed free of charge to essential services and front-line staff.

AWARDS

Since winning awards for Victoria Gin in 2016, the company has focused on submitting its best-selling Empress 1908 to various competitions. It won gold with distinction at the 2019 Canadian Artisan Spirit Competition, as well as a silver medal at the 2019 World Gin Awards. The San Diego International Wine & Spirits Challenge awarded it double gold in 2018. In 2017 the blue gin won gold at the New York World Wine & Spirits Competition and was named Best Alcohol Drink at the World Beverage Innovation Awards.

TOURS

Victoria Distillers offers tours and tastings at its Sidney premises. Check the website for open hours.

FAVOURITE COCKTAILS

THE ROYAL TREATMENT

4 oz (120 mL) white cranberry juice

1½ oz (45 mL) Victoria Gin or Empress 1908
  Gin

Sparkling wine

Kiwi slices, skin removed

Raspberries

Blackberries

6 mint leaves

Build in a stemless wineglass. Garnish with
the kiwi slices, berries, and mint.

THE DV 15

1½ oz (45 mL) Victoria Gin or Empress 1908 Gin

½ oz (15 mL) fresh lemon juice

½ oz (15 mL) simple syrup (1:1 sugar and water)

Sparkling wine

Shake the gin, lemon juice, and simple syrup
with ice. Pour into a champagne flute. Top with
sparkling wine. Rim the glass with citrus and
garnish with a twist.

THE ALWAYS POPULAR NEGRONI

1 oz (30 mL) Victoria Gin or Oaken Gin

½ oz (15 mL) Campari

½ oz (15 mL) sweet vermouth

Orange twist

Stir on ice, pour into a rocks glass with ice, and garnish with an orange twist.

AND FINALLY, A PLAY ON WORDS: VICTORIA'S SECRET

2 oz (60 mL) Victoria Gin

1½ oz (45 mL) fresh lemon juice

1 egg white

½ oz (15 mL) maple syrup

½ tsp (2.5 mL) freshly grated ginger

1 pinch fresh cilantro

1 pinch freshly ground pepper

Muddle the ingredients and shake with ice. Strain into a martini glass. Garnish with pepper.

COWICHAN
VALLEY REGION

8
MERRIDALE CIDERY & DISTILLERY

RICK PIPES AND JANET DOCHERTY, OWNERS

1230 MERRIDALE ROAD

PO BOX 358

COBBLE HILL, V0R 1L0

250-743-4293, TOLL-FREE 1-800-998-9908

INFO@MERRIDALE.CA

MERRIDALE.CA

LATITUDE 48.664500, LONGITUDE -123.586934

MORE THAN 20 YEARS AGO RICK PIPES AND JANET Docherty bought Merridale Cidery, and the family business has increased cider sales from 18,000 litres to more than 200,000 litres annually. That's important not only for cider making but also because the juice from fruit grown on the 20-acre property forms the base of all but one of Merridale's core spirits. Not a grain of barley or wheat in sight.

You might think that the couple have agricultural or farm backgrounds, but Rick was practising law and Janet was a commercial real estate agent when they bought Merridale from Al Piggott. "I provide the products for Janet to sell," says Rick. "We have a clear distinction in our roles that plays to both our strengths. Janet is a great marketer."

"We have a common business philosophy that allows us to reach our business and life goals," adds Janet. "We ask how we can farm sustainably so that the property can still be used a century from now."

Rick Pipes and Janet Docherty, owners of Merridale Cidery & Distillery.

To remain sustainable, Merridale uses no pesticides or herbicides. The ciders and spirits are not fermented or stored long term in plastic totes, which can taint the liquids. "Only glass, stainless steel, or wood," says Rick. The firm focuses on packaging that balances product quality, consumer aesthetics and safety, and the environment.

"We don't sell stuff as quickly as we can," adds Rick. "Many products rest, mellow, or mature, some for years. Quick fixes are usually not sustainable. And our staff must be intrinsically motivated by sustainability. Those are the people we keep."

The spent cider is spread in the orchards, as it still con-

Merridale's owners, Rick Pipes and Janet Docherty, with distiller Laurent Lafuente.

tains nutrients. Merridale has sustainable clean water from the 85-metre-deep well on the property. It's UV filtered but unchlorinated. The well water was bench tested and compared with water filtered by osmosis and other kinds of purified water. After the test, the well water was the purest and tasted the best, Merridale maintains.

Over the last two decades, Rick and Janet have improved the orchards carpeted with their well-pruned, mossy, English, German, and French cider apple trees. They have added buildings to the grounds that house the cider works, distillery, tasting bar, Merridale Eatery, farm store, events, and even yurts that serve as a glamorous retreat. Many weddings are held here as well. The grounds are beautiful and fertile. Merridale employs about 25 staff in the winter, and from 45 to 50 in the summer. It's agri-tourism at its best.

The cidery/distillery is located in Cobble Hill, in the Cowichan district, which takes its name from the Indigenous word Quw'utsun, meaning "the Warm Land." Surrounded by mountains and flanked by hilly islands, Cowichan is among the warmest regions in Canada by average annual temperature (9.2°C/48.5°F) and thus highly suitable for local, value-added agriculture. It's the right terroir for growing cider apples and grapes, as the growing season is long and slow. As the desire for local, small-batch, organic produce and products has grown, Cowichan farms, orchards, and vineyards have become popular destinations for culinary travel.

"We grow 10 varieties of cider apples," says Rick. "They originated in England, France, and Germany and have served as cider apples for centuries. Let me remind you, though, these apples are designed specifically for cider. They're astringent. You can't eat them like a Pink Lady or a Gala apple."

These apples will become part of Merridale's cider, and then spirits.

As the apples ripen at different times depending on their location on the tree and their exposure to the sun, each apple tree is harvested several times in late summer and fall.

THE BUSINESS PLAN

After buying the orchard, Rick continued his law practice for several years while the cidery improved its premises, sales, and cash flow. Janet, with her long business experience, took on the presidency and continues to manage the business affairs. Rick focuses on the products the orchard produces. Merridale has also become a multigenerational family business. Son Jason Child began with cider deliveries, moved to sales and, after a decade working many roles, now serves as general manager.

"In the beginning, we built sweat equity," Rick explains. "Piggott, the previous owner, was a Scot and a retired shop teacher. He was creative in making old equipment work, but it required constant maintenance, which limited production. His approach was highly labour intensive. We're still using some of his stuff but have also modernized. But we still cork bottles manually."

As the cidery grew and became more profitable, Rick added a distillery, called the Brandy House. "A new toy," he says, grinning. Thus, in 2007, six years before the BC government created laws allowing craft distilleries to establish themselves, Merridale obtained a licence for a commercial distillery, the only licence available at the time. It was the same year that Ken Winchester founded Winchester Spirits and launched Victoria Gin. That company is now called Victoria Distillers (see chapter 7).

Rick tells me some of the background that eventually led to legislation allowing craft distilleries to be established in British Columbia. It took years of lobbying. Rick teamed with Frank Deiter, then owner of Okanagan Spirits (now representing Müller stills), and they never stopped talking to government officials about changing the laws and regulations. They pointed out the similarities between craft brewing and craft distilling, noted that other provinces were issuing licences, and showed that US craft distillers were making an impact on agriculture and creating consumer enthusiasm. "Frank is the granddad of distilling in BC, I'm the young cousin," says Rick.

"Because I used only BC ingredients and made small batches, I was already a craft distiller, but the rules forced me into a commercial distillery classification," Rick continues. "The irony was that I couldn't sell my products to the BC Liquor Distribution Branch, as the fees and markups are so huge I couldn't break even, let alone make a profit." After the 2013 craft distillery laws took effect, Merridale became BC's first full-fledged craft distillery. Rick says he helped write the audit rules regulating craft distilleries and was the first to be audited.

Merridale has plans to expand to Victoria West, on a property that oversees the Point Hope shipyards in downtown Victoria. It's an active area with much housing construction, a large shopping centre, and views of a lively, working harbour.

The plan is to build a grain-based distillery with a cocktail lounge open to the distilling area containing two stills: a 100-year-old copper still, the Princess, now housed at the Cobble Hill farm's gazebo, that will make gin; and a multifunctional still focusing on vodka and whisky production. As is true with all alcohol-related premises, a distiller must clear many hurdles with various levels of government before licences are granted.

MERRIDALE'S DISTILLING PROCESS

To add distilling expertise to his knowledge of cider making, Rick took distilling courses in Vermont and at the University of Michigan. One day a week, Laurent Lafuente, a master-distiller consultant and a Swiss-trained French winemaker with vast experience in distilling and blending, visits Merridale and, with Rick, distills in the distilling room with its tasting bar. (I met Laurent first when he consulted and taught distilling at Phillips Fermentorium; he has helped several distilleries get started.) The distillery occupies part of a building that also houses a series of huge cider-fermenting vats.

The distillery's centrepiece is a 200-litre, hand-hammered, copper Müller Brennerei pot still made in Oberkirch, Germany. It's an uncommon still, as it's wood fired—the only operational one among the 21 distilleries in this book (Victoria Distillers has a wood-fired still but rarely uses it). While I visited, Laurent Lafuente was feeding chunks of pine into the still's firebox while cider was percolating in the still in a stripping run. "We use fairly small pieces of wood," says Rick, "so we can control the fire's heat."

I ask Rick why he chose a wood-fired still. "It's the Porsche of stills," he says. "In the history of distilling, it's always been known that equipment influences the product. I like this particular still. We know distilling processes are varied and individual. Not everyone likes the same style. It's like paintings. Some like Monet; others like Picasso."

Merridale's wood-fired still.

Pure alcohol drips from the still's condenser.

Merridale has released only a single cask of whisky with a malted-barley base. (They branded it Whisky Jack's in honour of Rick's and Janet's fathers, both whisky lovers and both named Jack.) Rick confesses he has a bias. "I'm not a Scotch drinker. It tastes like hooch to me, like moonshine. I concentrate on different spirits. In the beginning, I tried distilling many kinds of fruit—cherries, pears, plums, apricots, peaches, apples. But I quickly learned I needed to focus. We always make cider, of course, and we distill pear into spirit if the weather favours us. Using fruit is about 10 times more expensive than grain. But that's what is at hand. We never rush any product to market. Our cidery's success gives us the luxury of time."

Merridale starts distilling with cider and makes five to six stripping runs through the pot still. "Distilling is not alchemy," says Rick. "What you need is good inputs, a properly fermented base. The first finished product from the still is a neutral spirit, which becomes Cowichan Vodka after it mellows in stainless vats and is then cold-filtered through activated charcoal."

Rick has strong views on the quality of casks in which his brandies mature. "The Scots are thrifty and import bourbon barrels from Kentucky. They cost about $200 each. A new barrel is about $1,200."

Generally, casks are used two or three times before they're retired. But Rick's taste runs to new casks. "Used bourbon casks have already used up 75 percent of their flavour and of their charred insides that neutralize the alcohol's harshness and sulphur compounds," he says forcefully, "even casks that have been recharred. But new, dense oak wood, lightly toasted, releases consistent flavour resins. Those resins are more available in new wood."

I walk over to a rack stacked with barrels. They look clean and new with just an occasional tiny streak of caramelized resins and alcohol seeping out from the dense staves. They're filled with apple and pear brandies. I look closely at one barrel. It's branded French Oak Medium Toast. A small paper is stapled into the wood: "Apple blend #2," it says. "November 2010, 66.4 percent ABV [alcohol by volume]."

Merridale's brandies are the oldest craft brandies in North America, Rick tells me. The apple and pear brandies mature at least six years in their casks. The casks are rotated regularly within the distillery, as those closer to the still experience warmer temperatures—a factor that can influence the spirits' flavour concentrations as well as increase the "angel's share," or evaporation. They often use a wine thief to taste-test the spirits, drawing up the liquid through the cask's bunghole.

Rick and Laurent blend the barrels with the same input product and reduce the alcohol content to its desired strength in stages to avoid chemical reactions. "We try all our products neat," says Rick. "We blend and taste so they're good enough to drink without mixes. We always look for authenticity. But, of course, they can be fused into smooth cocktails as well."

In the tasting room, Rick demonstrates how to taste a spirit properly. "First, you waft your hand over the glass and take a

Some of Merridale's products. Courtesy Merridale.

small whiff, then a good sniff. Wet your lips with the liquid, followed by a little taste, then a full sip. You'll get a burst of aroma and flavour."

MERRIDALE'S SPIRITS

Cowichan Vodka uses Merridale's cider as its base. After it's distilled, it's filtered through activated charcoal and then redistilled. Next, the spirit mellows for about two to three years in stainless steel vats and is then again cold-filtered through charcoal. The alcohol by volume is 40 percent.

Cowichan Gin uses two-to-three-year-old neutral spirits made from Merridale cider. It is infused with a prodigious number of botanicals—more than 40 wild and native botanicals foraged from the Cowichan Valley. The following ingredient list is but a sample: juniper, apple blossom and skins, rosemary, cucumber peel, dandelion root, devil's club, basil, fresh cedar tips, and rhubarb leaves. "None of these ingredients dominate," says Rick. "It's a gentle gin, made for non-gin drinkers." The alcohol by volume is 47 percent.

Copper Gin transforms Cowichan Gin by maturing it in Pinot Noir casks supplied by local wineries. Before it enters the casks, the gin's flavour is enhanced by macerated juniper, orange peel, and cardamom. It makes for a hardier, more robust flavour. The alcohol by volume is 47 percent.

Cowichan Cider Brandy is again made from the base of Merridale's cider apples, using six specially chosen varieties to create a distinctive flavour profile. Once distilled, the spirit is aged in new French oak barrels for a minimum of six years. It's recommended to drink this brandy at room temperature, after swirling it gently in a snifter. The alcohol by volume is 42 percent.

Cowichan XXO Brandy mixes white and red grapes from a single Okanagan Valley vineyard. Merridale has made only one batch and one barrel of this robust brandy. After being double-distilled, this spirit rested for 10 years in a new French oak barrel. Even the barrel is made in BC. The alcohol by volume is 47 percent.

Stair's Pear Brandy uses fermented Bartlett pears as its base. "We think this is North America's oldest barrel-aged pear brandy," says Rick. "Each sip reminds you of biting into a fresh pear just picked from the tree, followed by that smooth warmth of a fine brandy." Wikipedia explains how this tipple received its name. It appears the first person to cultivate this type of pear was a British school headmaster, John Stairs. He grew this pear in his schoolyard in the 1760s, and it became known as "Stair's pear." A tree nursery worker by the name of Williams acquired the variety, and the fruit was rechristened as "Williams pear" after it spread across the British Isles. James Carter imported the pear in 1799 for planting in a Massachusetts estate, which was later acquired by one Enoch Bartlett. He named the fruit after himself. By calling Merridale's pear brandy after Headmaster Stairs, the firm honours the memory of this historic pear variety grower. The alcohol by volume is 47 percent.

Whisky Jack's is Merridale's single cask of whisky, made from organic malted barley and aged for seven years in a French oak barrel. The spirit's name was bestowed in memory of Rick's and Janet's fathers, both named Jack, who both enjoyed a wee dram of whisky before dinner. It is no longer for sale.

If you're a sailor, you will plot a rhumb line on your chart. It's a straight line drawn to reach your destination as quickly as possible (weather permitting, of course). Merridale chose the

The gazebo surrounded by apple trees at Merridale.

name Cowichan Rhumb "to reflect the firm's steadiness in keeping its bearings through years of challenges to produce this truly Cowichan version of rum" as they explain on their website. To maintain the "craft distillery" standing, Merridale couldn't use imported molasses to make rum, so it bought BC honey, fermented it, and double-distilled the wash. The result has aged in new French oak barrels for at least one year. The alcohol by volume is 43 percent.

Cowichan Spiced Rhumb is Cowichan Rhumb that has been flavoured with vanilla, cinnamon, molasses, and other Caribbean spices. To infuse these flavours, the distillers insert a macerating tube into a cask's bunghole. The tube is filled with small pieces of the macerated botanicals that infuse the rum. The alcohol by volume is 43 percent.

Apple Oh de Vie (a brandy) is made from Merridale's cider and then aged in French oak barrels. The distillery makes only very limited quantities of this elixir because it's made from a special blend of French and English cider apples. It's often quaffed as a digestif or in martinis.

Merridale also produces two fortified tipples, each with an alcohol by volume of 19.5 percent. Oaked Harvest Cider combines apple cider and brandy into a slightly sweet drink. In the tradition of Normandy and Brittany, fresh-pressed cider apples are fermented in French oak barrels. At the right moment, Merridale's cider brandy is added, which stops the fermentation and preserves the natural sweetness of the apples. The fortified spirit continues to age until it reaches maturity.

Apple Dessert Cider is also called "apple pie in a bottle." It's made completely differently from the Oaked Harvest Cider. It begins with a balanced blend of Merridale's favourite cider apples. It ferments while more food is added to keep the yeast fed. The yeast is forced to ferment the cider up to 17 percent and beyond. Then, the cider ages and relaxes in a stainless steel tank. A year later, additional apple juice and a small amount of Apple Oh de Vie bring it up to 19 percent alcohol by volume. The resulting fortified cider resembles an apple port, with an aroma of baked apples. It can be poured like port. Merridale recommends pairing it with cheddar or blue cheese, melons, fruit desserts, and dark chocolate.

AWARDS

With one exception, Merridale has submitted its products to the Canadian Artisan Spirit Competition to be judged. In 2020, the company won gold medals for its Cowichan Cider Brandy and Cowichan Spiced Rhumb, and silver medals for its Cowichan Cherry Brandy, Cowichan Rhumb and Cowichan Gin. In addition, Merridale's Cowichan Pear Brandy was awarded a gold medal in the Aged Brandy category at the 2014 American Distilling Institute Spirit Competition.

TOURS AND EVENTS

Merridale participates in wine and spirit festivals. Its website regularly lists its upcoming events. Canadian Craft Tours, Vancouver Island Expeditions, and Cheers Cowichan Tours all include Merridale in their Cowichan-area culinary tours.

SIGNATURE COCKTAILS

HONEY BEE

Fresh ginger
1 oz (30 mL) Cowichan Gin
1 oz (30 mL) Hop Honey Simple Syrup
½ oz (15 mL) fresh lemon juice
2 dashes Angostura Bitters
Cyser Cider

Muddle fresh ginger in a cocktail shaker and add ice, then the other ingredients. Shake vigorously and strain into a 14 oz glass with ice. Top with Merridale Cyser Cider.

TIKI TIME

1 oz (30 mL) Cowichan Rhumb

1 oz (30 mL) Rosemary Cinnamon Simple Syrup

½ oz (15 mL) fresh lime juice

2 dashes Peychaud's Bitters

Merri Berri Cider

Place in a shaker with ice and shake vigorously. Strain into a 14 oz glass with ice and top with Merridale Merri Berri Cider.

ELIXIR DE VIE

1 oz (30 mL) Oaked Harvest Cider

½ oz (15 mL) Cowichan Cider Brandy

½ oz (15 mL) fresh-pressed apple juice

½ oz (15 mL) Merridale cider gastrique

Combine in a shaker with ice and shake vigorously. Strain into a martini glass.

9
GOLDSTREAM DISTILLERY

KATHLEEN AND DARCY TRINGHAM AND COLIN
    CUMBERBATCH, CO-OWNERS

4A–4715 TRANS-CANADA HIGHWAY (HIGHWAY 19),
    WHIPPLETREE JUNCTION

8A WHIPPLETREE FRONTAGE ROAD

DUNCAN, BC V9L 6E1

250-213-8476

INFO@GOLDSTREAMDISTILLERY.COM

GOLDSTREAMDISTILLERY.COM

LATITUDE 48.739849, LONGITUDE -123.653483

Goldstream Distillery's owners, Kathleen and Darcy Tringham and Colin Cumberbatch.

GOLDSTREAM DISTILLERY OPERATES IN A remarkable development about 15 kilometres south of Duncan. A hodgepodge of salvaged shops forms a small community with a long pedigree. Whippletree Junction is made up of some of the buildings from Duncan's former Chinatown and a variety of other structures that were brought here from Cobble Hill and Sooke. It had become mostly an antique mall but has started to diversify. Goldstream Distillery occupies one corner of a series of small shops. Its distilling and bottling equipment is positioned in a single large room, accompanied by an alcove for boxed spirits. The owners hope to acquire an additional space next door to serve as a tasting room and retail store.

Darcy and Kathleen Tringham and Colin Cumberbatch distill their vodka and gin only on weekends, as they all work full-time. Colin owns Cornerstone Mechanical, a plumbing and HVAC company. Appropriately, his work has included installing the water and heating systems at Sooke Oceanside Brewery and at Bad Dog Brewing Company, both in Sooke, and at Black Hops, a Victoria brewery run by veterans. He is Goldstream's head distiller and also manages the spirit maker's mechanical needs.

Kathleen now works in home insurance but has used her past retail management experience to market and sell Goldstream's spirits. "I sold 99 percent of our spirits through direct personal contact," she says. "I have poured our quarter ounces of vodka and gin in BC Liquor Stores and private liquor shops. Interestingly, about one in six customers would buy a bottle of our spirits after the taste test."

Darcy works for a building supply company and manages the logistics for distributing these supplies. He also uses these skills in the distillery, handling procurement, keeping the books, and ensuring the spirits get to the liquor stores.

The Tringhams and Colin have been friends for at least three decades. Darcy had been home brewing beer in his garage. "It was legal to brew beer," he says. "I made it from scratch, using hops and live yeast. I always wanted to try distilling but knew it was illegal."

OBTAINING THE DISTILLING LICENCE

Goldstream secured its distilling licence in a manner different from all the other distilleries on Vancouver Island and the Gulf Islands. Darcy tells me he and Kathleen were visiting Salt Spring Island to celebrate a birthday when serendipity struck. They spotted a local newspaper advertisement offering a distillery with a commercial licence for sale in Campbell River. The distillery had never opened for business. The Tringhams conferred with Colin, and they agreed that a ready-made distillery presented a great business opportunity.

The trio bought the distillery's equipment and its 2018 spirit licence with their own funds. "Getting a licence transferred rarely happens," says Darcy, "although we still had to jump through many hoops." They retained the name the original distillery owner had bestowed, Goldstream. "That was also part of the serendipity," says Darcy. "We all live close to Goldstream and the provincial park just north of Victoria." (The area is called Goldstream because, for a short period in 1863, miners thought gold could be sluiced from the stream. They were wrong.)

After the paperwork was completed and the Duncan location secured, the team moved the distillery and its contents to Whippletree Junction and ensured the still, bottler, and other equipment were properly installed and operational. Colin's

Goldstream's Vodka. Photo: Jason Salisbury.

plumbing and HVAC experience was a serious advantage. The 200-litre column still they acquired in the purchase was fabricated by North Stills, based in Toronto. The still can be converted to a pot still by installing a copper column piece and/or a copper hood.

They launched their first spirits in April 2019. The artisan distillery orders its neutral grain spirits, distilled from wheat, from Alberta. The spirits arrive in totes. Colin started distilling having gained much information from the internet. "I didn't want to reinvent the wheel," he says. "But getting formal training would have been costly and time consuming. And besides, I like to learn by myself."

"It isn't all that different from brewing beer," adds Darcy. "I brewed beer by feel. But for our spirits, Colin and I worked out a recipe so that we can distill a consistent spirit."

They started off distilling four small batches, writing down each step in the process. After much tasting, they chose batch number four. Then they scaled up to ensure they could replicate the vodka's flavour in larger quantities. When satisfied with the results—"Our distilling plan is different from other small-batch distilleries"—they began researching the methods and ingredients to produce gin. "Making vodka is science," says Darcy. "Making gin is a transition to art. It's like painting a canvas. It's unique."

"Yes," adds Kathleen, "it's more fun than work when you know you've chosen the right method and ingredients."

Kathleen notes that every bottle is made with passion and love. "People have told me they don't know how the bottle got empty." She credits their triple-distilled vodka's "shocking smoothness" partly to the well water supply. They tested the water and found trace amounts of gold in the water. "We filter our water and run it through a UV system," she adds. "But our water's mineral content flavours our spirits differently."

Goldstream's gin is made in two stages. First the botanicals, juniper (grown in Macedonia) and Canadian coriander, are soaked in vodka for a week. Then the flavoured spirit is redistilled with a stainless steel basket placed in the still's column. The basket contains cinnamon chips, angelica root, orrisroot, cubeb pepper, licorice, grains of paradise, and grapefruit. They call it "hybrid distilling."

Botanicals for gin.

Although plastic is inevitable in today's manufacturing, Colin is especially dedicated to fighting plastics in the distilling equipment. "When you put hot ethanol through plastic bulkhead fittings, it will degrade the plastic and enter your spirits and, eventually, the person drinking the spirits. I've installed only marine-grade, 316-grade stainless fittings, although they cost 10 times more than plastic ones. And the hoses need to be silicone."

In the future, the team plans to add whisky and rum to their repertoire. "We already have a proof of concept in hand," says Darcy. "Once we have enough volume, we hope to quit our jobs and run the business full-time."

Distiller Colin Cumberbatch.

GOLDSTREAM'S PRODUCTS

Goldstream Vodka is exceptionally smooth according to its website; one can drink it straight or mix it with tonic or other cocktail ingredients. It can be purchased at 46 BC Liquor Stores and about 30 private liquor stores. Alcohol by volume is 40 percent.

Goldstream Gin begins its life as Goldstream Vodka and is flavoured by the nine botanicals described earlier. At the time this book went to press, the gin was available only on-site. Alcohol by volume is 40 percent.

Along with other craft distilleries, Goldstream began making hand sanitizer during the COVID-19 pandemic. Its Goldstream Clean Golden Hand Sanitizer was made available to first responders, hospitals, and grocery stores.

10
STILLHEAD DISTILLERY

BRENNAN COLEBANK, CO-OWNER WITH FAMILY
     MEMBERS

#105, 5301 CHASTER ROAD

DUNCAN, BC V9L 0G4

250-748-6874

ORDERS@STILLHEAD.CA

STILLHEAD.CA

LATITUDE 48.764473, LONGITUDE -123.693001

Bird's-eye view of Stillhead Distillery. Courtesy Stillhead.

AMONG THE DISTILLERS ON VANCOUVER ISLAND
and the Gulf Islands, several have radically changed their careers
from more conventional ones to the more rarefied one of making
spirits. Rick Pipes at Merridale substituted lawyering for cider
and spirit making, Leon Webb renounced international banking
for the creativity of distilling spirits at Shelter Point, and Brennan
Colebank bowed out of IT work to found his own craft distillery.

Brennan, a tall, solid guy with a well-trimmed dark beard and a Stillhead-logoed baseball cap firmly in place, grew up in Prince George and completed his computer science degree at the University of Northern British Columbia. It seemed like a worthwhile degree in our electronic age, and Brennan ran the IT desk for a contractor to the BC government for 13 years. One day, however, he resolved there would be "no more travel" away from his wife, Erika, and his son and daughter. "I'd always loved whisky," he tells me in his Duncan-based distillery. "I'd studied a lot of chemistry at university, but when I graduated in 2004, distilling was not a career path.

"Once BC began issuing craft distilling licences in 2013, it was my wife, Erika Colebank, who suggested we start a distillery. She knew I liked making spirits and believed we could find success, like Ampersand and [Salt Spring] Shine. 'It's a good idea,' she told me."

Giving up a well-paying job to become an entrepreneur with substantial start-up equipment costs is not for the faint hearted. When I ask Brennan about the distillery's business plan, his answer is honest and short: "I make spirits; Erika makes the money."

Erika is a denturist, and her skills are very portable—an advantage when the family moved to Duncan. Brennan's

Stillhead's premises. Courtesy Stillhead.

parents, Ron and Christal Colebank, also became partners, so Stillhead has four owners—making the craft distillery another family-invested venture. "I saved up, and we all pooled our funds," says Brennan. In the early days, Brennan's parents worked about half time at Stillhead, but now that the operation is on solid legs, they spend about one-quarter of their time there.

"I had a hard time getting a proper location for the distillery," Brennan adds. "It took a while." He explains there are many provincial and municipal requirements for distilleries to operate and that most buildings are unsuitable. The zoning must allow the production of spirits—at a minimum, that means it must be situated away from residential areas. The building must be large and high enough to place stills, install fermenters, store casks, and house bottling equipment and product. It must be hooked up to proper sewers and to code-certified electrical and natural gas services. Extensive fireproofing is another requisite.

"I started working on the rezoning process in 2015," Brennan says. "It took two years to finally get all the permits. After jumping through the hoops, we started distilling in August 2017 and had our formal opening two months later."

How did Brennan decide on the name of his distillery? I ask if it was a takeoff on "whisky head" or "peat head."

"No," he responds. "The Stillhead name is a double entendre on *still* and *steelhead*, the fish that returns annually to the Cowichan River." Brennan is a fisherman and is concerned about steelheads' health. "They're like the canary in the mine," he says. "The Cowichan River, a BC Heritage River since 2003, is famous for this fish, but if there's environmental trouble,

Brennan Colebank prepares a flight of cocktails. Courtesy Stillhead.

they're the first to disappear." The steelhead is part of the distillery's logo and is also branded on the casks of maturing whisky.

The company's packaging features the same label for each spirit, but in differing hues. All labels feature Stillhead's circular, flowing water motif with a steelhead swimming upstream.

Stillhead has a nifty copper-covered tasting bar displaying its products and jars of botanicals that flavour its gin. Behind the bar, racks support a bevy of barrels, all marked with the contents and year they were laid up.

THE ART OF DISTILLING

Although Brennan had long been enticed by the art and science of distilling, he wanted more formal training. "I didn't do my research on the internet," he says. "It's full of bad advice." Instead, he attended a week-long "boot camp" taught by the Canadian Craft Distilling Institute at Kelowna's Urban Distilleries. "It was distilling 101, extremely hands-on," says Brennan. "They use the on-site Arnold Holstein pot and column stills as part of the instruction."

The workshop led Brennan to explore Arnold Holstein's stills for his own distillery. The German firm has a solid reputation for quality and has been manufacturing distilling and ancillary equipment for more than 60 years. "I got hooked on Holstein equipment," says Brennan. "I bought a 500-litre pot and column still." The equipment, with the usual copper and stainless steel exterior, gleams in front of the main window. "It worked out well because the North American partner and distributor for the firm, Dr. Lewis Harsanyi, actually came to Duncan for 10 days," Brennan continues. "We focused on the equipment and how to

*Brennan Colebank
by his stills.*

Maturing whisky with its angel's share.

use it for maximum effectiveness while distilling. I also spent four days in his Los Angeles–area shop. This intense support was most useful."

Brennan is convinced that the fermentation process is more important than distilling. "Once you have a good-quality wash, the still doesn't matter as much. We all use similar yeast, but the kind of fermenter we use, how we heat and cool the mash, the yeast's hydration and oxygenation, the nutrients, those are the important aspects for me. It takes careful monitoring to ensure the mash and wash are top quality."

Stillhead's fermenters and mash tuns have been supplied by Bavarian Breweries & Distilleries, another German company with a long pedigree (this company partners with Holstein). I ask Brennan why he chose these particular vats. "Because they're awesome," he says enthusiastically. "This company also has long experience fabricating tuns and fermenters, and their support for us craft distillers is amazing."

When I visited the distillery, I watched as the grain bubbled in the mash tuns. It created a pleasantly warm environment on a cold, rainy day, and the sweet, piquant aroma of cooking barley perfumed the air.

Mike Feld has joined Stillhead as head distiller, and the operation runs full out five days a week. The vodka and gin are made from 100 percent unmalted wheat, with added yeast and enzymes to convert the starch to sugar. "I make vodka for people who don't like gin," says Brennan. "Vodka is the 'white wall' of spirits. The unmalted wheat base gives it its mild flavour so appropriate for cocktails."

Stillhead has also been laying up whiskies using a variety of grains, showing that Vancouver Island craft distillers are innovating beyond the standard malted-barley base and stepping outside the strict rules governing Scottish or Irish whiskey makers.

"We've been making whisky for three and a half years," says Brennan. "Right now, we have nearly 150 barrels maturing on-site and in a warehouse. We're continually adding to our stock. Some of our casks are filled with 100 percent rye grain whisky, others whiskies are distilled from 100 percent malted barley, and a third group contains a mixed base of corn, malted barley, and rye. Some of our casks are one-offs. All our grains are supplied by South Peace Grain in Dawson Creek and grown in BC."

The casks that Brennan has purchased include new American oak casks, casks that once contained maturing bourbon, and wine barrels. "I must tell you that buying casks is the issue I lose the most sleep over," he says. "I obtain them from a barrel broker, but they're ever harder to buy as the craft distillery explosion continues. The price tag increases along with the competition. And shipping costs are brutal. Right now an ex-bourbon cask costs about US$200 and a new American oak cask runs about US$250. And shipping costs are on top of that."

STILLHEAD'S PRODUCTS

Unlike most distilleries, Stillhead makes its vodka out of 100 percent malted wheat instead of the usual barley, which gives the vodka a "sweeter" taste. Its packaging features the flowing water motif with blue swirls. The alcohol by volume is 40 percent.

Stillhead's gin has its start as vodka and is made in the traditional London dry style. It's double-distilled and flavoured with juniper, angelica, coriander, cassia, cubeb, cardamom, star anise, and a combo of lemon and lime peel. Brennan says it's "specially tailored to be used in a gin martini or any classic cocktail." The gin label's swirls are golden, and the alcohol by volume is 43 percent.

Stillhead's Barrel-Aged Gin has matured in an ex-bourbon cask for one year, infusing oak flavours into the spirit. It's a limited-edition product with an alcohol-by-volume content of 43 percent.

Wild Blackberry Vodka is Stillhead's best-selling spirit and capitalizes on BC's enormous quantities of blackberry canes that colonize fields, streams, and roadway berms. It's an organic fruit—no one sprays or fertilizes it—but as it grows wild, it's not certified.

In the summer, when the fruit is at its peak, Indigenous Cowichan Bay people pick about 5,500 kilograms of blackberries in six days. To retain freshness, Brennan freezes the berries in

The botanicals Stillhead uses to flavour gin.

blocks and stores them in a big on-site freezer. The berries are juiced and then steeped in vodka. The spirit contains no additives or added sugars. It's available all year—unless it sells out and Brennan has to defrost some berries to make the next batch. Its flowing water label is an appropriate deep mauve colour. The alcohol by volume is 35 percent.

Aged Apple Brandy is a seasonal release. It's made from fresh, chopped Okanagan Ambrosia apples that are fermented. It takes nine pounds of apples to make the liquor that fills one 375-millilitre bottle. After distillation, the apple-scented spirit slumbers in oak casks that previously held maple syrup. It's a delicious mix of small-batch vodka, BC apples, and one of Canada's most iconic products—maple syrup. The alcohol by volume is 40 percent.

Stillhead's Cask Club is for whisky lovers who wish to choose their private cask's content and monitor it as it matures. The cask's wood and previous alcohol content will, of course, influence their spirit over time, and thus each barrel owner will have a uniquely flavoured whisky. Barrels come in 30-litre and 5-litre sizes. The 30-litre cask ages in the distillery until it's ready for bottling. The 5-litre cask goes home with the Cask Club buyer.

The choice of whiskies are Canadian rye, made from 80 percent rye and 20 percent malted barley; bourbon style, made from a blend of corn, barley, and rye; and single malt, made from 100 percent malted barley.

During the COVID-19 pandemic, Stillhead joined other craft distillers in making hand sanitizer. The recipe was based on the World Health Organization's recommendations: 80 percent alcohol-based hand rub. It also contained hydrogen peroxide to prevent people from drinking the sanitizer.

AWARDS

Stillhead has won several awards, but Brennan doesn't sign up for many contests. "They're expensive and there's a lot of paperwork, plus fees, especially if you're sending your samples to be evaluated in the US," he says. That said, Stillhead products have won awards at the SIP Awards in Los Angeles (platinum for London Dry Gin, silver for Prime 1 Vodka) and at the Northwest Wine Summit (gold for Wild Blackberry Vodka).

TOURS AND MARKETS

Stillhead hosts a tasting bar where both locals and tourists visit and try a few sips. For summer and winter hours, consult stillhead.ca.

The distillery sells its spirits at Moss Street Market in Victoria, the Cobble Hill and Duncan farmers' markets in the Cowichan Valley, and the Prince George farmers' market.

FAVOURITE COCKTAILS

MOSCOW MULE

2 oz (60 mL) Stillhead Vodka

Ginger beer

Slice of lime

Sprig of mint

Pour the vodka into a copper mug, julep tin, or tumbler. Load ¾ full with crushed ice. Top with ginger beer and stir gently to combine. Garnish with a slice of lime and a sprig of mint.

CUCUMBER COLLINS

2 oz (60 mL) Stillhead London Dry Gin

1 oz (30 mL) fresh lemon juice

1 oz (30 mL) simple syrup (1:1 sugar and water)

Handful cucumber chunks

Soda water

Cucumber slice

Shake with ice, then strain over ice in a glass. Top with soda water and garnish with a cucumber slice.

BLACKBERRY SPLASH

½ oz (15 mL) Stillhead Vodka
½ oz (15 mL) Stillhead Wild Blackberry Vodka
½ oz (15 mL) fresh lemon juice
½ oz (15 mL) simple syrup (1:1 sugar and water)
Soda water

Shake the vodkas, lemon juice, and simple syrup well with ice. Pour over ice and top with soda water.

11
AMPERSAND DISTILLING COMPANY

STEPHEN SCHACHT, RAMONA FROEHLE-SCHACHT,
JEREMY SCHACHT, AND JESSICA SCHACHT
CO-OWNERS

4077 LANCHASTER ROAD

DUNCAN, BC V9L 6G2

250-999-1109

INFO@AMPERSANDDISTILLING.COM

AMPERSANDDISTILLING.COM

LATITUDE 48.766079, LONGITUDE -123.779449

AMPERSAND DISTILLING COMPANY IS A TRUE FAMILY affair with two generations of Schachts working together creatively to make their spirits. It includes the parents, Stephen and Ramona, their son, Jeremy, and his wife, Jessica. The patriarch, Stephen, told me what a privilege it is that at his age of 76, he can work in a close relationship with his wife, son, and daughter-in-law.

To reflect the collaborative, symbiotic family skills, they named their company after the phrase "and per se &," a term later slurred together into the word *ampersand*. We are all familiar with the symbol &. It's the logogram that stands for *and*, and is frequently used to connect the names of business partners, as in Johnson & Johnson, or in abbreviations such as B&B.

The idea of creating a distillery was fomented by Jeremy and Jessica, who had enjoyed the burgeoning cocktail culture during their student years. Jessica majored in theatre management at the University of Victoria and deploys her creative side in labelling, advertising, and marketing Ampersand's spirits, while Jeremy earned a degree in applied chemical engineering from the University of British Columbia. "It gave me a technical background and an interest in distilling," he says.

Jeremy had gained experience working in a chemical plant during his third university year. "With these studies, you mostly end up in oil and gas," he says. "It's not an industry that particularly attracted me." After graduation, he worked as a deckhand at Harbour Air and paid off his student loans. But the couple yearned to do something creative, something entrepreneurial.

Jeremy and Jessica approached Stephen and Ramona with the idea of launching a distillery. Stephen is an engineer and inventor. He and Ramona already owned a five-acre organic vegetable farm they'd bought in Cowichan Valley in 2007. They liked

Stephen Schacht, Ramona Froehle-Schacht, and Jeremy Schacht.

the distillery concept and teamed up with the next generation. "We developed a robust, three-year business plan," Jeremy says. "We forecast how we could develop over several years and were able to borrow a small amount of cash." Once they met their production goals, Alex Palmer joined the company as a full-time distiller.

A PERFECT LOCATION

Ampersand officially opened in 2014, as one of the earliest distilleries in BC to have gained the craft licence to make small-batch vodka and gin. The farm already owned a sizable workshop that was adapted to the distillery's needs. Being isolated in a rural area made it easier to obtain the necessary provincial and municipal zoning permits.

Ampersand Distilling Company building.

The distillery differs from others in that a good part of its equipment was hand built, including the shelving and tasting bar. "We certainly started out doing everything ourselves," says Jeremy, "but we've tried to streamline it." They built their own stills, buying the pot and column still components from a Vancouver company. "We ordered four-foot-diameter domes to make double-bottomed pots, where we can inject steam from a boiler and bring it to the required temperature for distilling." Jeremy welded the pieces together. "I donned my welding mask and spent days inside the pot stills," says Jeremy. "I learned a lot about welding and also how to rig up a clean air supply so as to not be stuck with the fumes inside a pot still!"

When the 500-litre and 1,000-litre copper and stainless steel stills—nicknamed Dot and Dash—were completed, Stephen surrounded them with insulating cedar slabs, held in place with stainless steel straps. The mash tun was similarly constructed by father and son and again clad with cedar planks. The warm

Ampersand's cedar-clad, hand-built distilling equipment.
Photo: Centric Photography.

wood coverings add elegance to the equipment. The single tall column—which extends into a square roof cupola—contains no windows and is packed with thousands of tiny stainless steel coils for maximum surface area; the coils make it simple for the distiller to separate the heads, hearts, and tails. "The stills make alcohol with a purity reaching a very high 96.5 percent," says Jeremy. "That's as high a distillation result as you can get." The variously sized stainless steel vats and 1,100-litre fermentation tanks were manufactured by Marchisio and Sansone in Italy.

Outside the distillery, two silos contain 28 tonnes of organic, soft white winter wheat that Ampersand uses to make its spirits. The grain is grown on several organic farms in the Armstrong, BC, area and is delivered twice a year. "It's tricky for the delivery truck to use its auger conveyor to get the grain into our tall silos," says Jeremy. "The silos deliver the grain to our

Ampersand's wheat silos.

mash tuns after it's cracked and milled."

Using Ampersand's own UV-treated well water, the distillers add two enzymes to maximize the breakdown of starch in the mash tun and add a proprietary yeast to the fermenters. "Alex makes the yeast happy," says Jeremy.

"Since 2014, we've optimized our process," he continues. "Using raw wheat and enzymes has made us more efficient. We're now on a six-day rotation of fermenting and the various steps of distilling. We get about 10 litres of head with the spirit run. These are used in biodiesel, and our spent grain is delivered to farms as animal feed. Our pure spring water tempers the spirits to the correct proof. We now produce about two thousand 750-millilitre bottles per month."

Since 2014, the Schachts have been attempting to grow as many of their gin botanicals as possible on their own farm. "The juniper still comes from Bulgaria," Ramona says. "The Balkans are prime growers of juniper. But we are cultivating our own orris-root, the root of an iris." It takes at least three years to

The organic, soft white winter wheat Ampersand uses for its spirits. Photo: Marc Phillips.

grow a full orrisroot; then it's dried and ground and added to gin. It maintains its floral notes after distillation. "It smells like Parma violets," says Ramona. "We are also trying to produce our own coriander seeds. And we grow wormwood for our Imperative Dry Vermouth."

INTERNATIONAL HELP

The family farm has joined World Wide Opportunities on Organic Farms, or WWOOF. It's an international program in which young adults from around the world can learn and work on an organic farm. They are not paid a salary, but they receive room and board with the sponsoring farm. "We've had about 100 young people from places like Germany, France, Italy, Australia, and Japan," says Ramona. "An organic farm is very labour intensive, and we can't afford to hire staff. They work a few hours every day, and thus the program allows us to do a bit of ad hoc hiring."

Ramona has long experience managing craft fairs, including Victoria's famous Out of Hand annual craft fair. She runs the stalls at four farmers' markets, handles taste testing in private liquor stores, and manages the many requests for spirit donations to charities and gala fundraisers. "We have a following," she says. "Local people like to buy local. But we also have customers from as far away as Manitoba, and when they visit BC, they buy cases of our spirits and divvy them up with their friends and neighbours at home. Snowbirds take our products with them. We even had one Ontarian buy a case and check it as luggage on their plane back home."

"Jeremy and I learned about distilled spirits through cocktail culture," Jessica says. "It's part of why running a distillery is so appealing. And it's great to be part of a craft group. It adds to the BC economy and supports local farmers. The regulations allow us to distribute directly, making the enterprise worthwhile financially. And it's a terrific way for young people to create their own jobs."

AMPERSAND'S PRODUCTS

Per Se Vodka is the distillery's first product to leave the still. Its 96 percent alcohol content is diluted with on-site well water. It's unfiltered. You can drink it straight or with a cocktail mix. Alcohol by volume is 40 percent.

The Ampersand Gin recipe was developed by Jessica and Jeremy. It starts with the highly purified Per Se Vodka and is flavoured with eight cultivated or wild harvested botanicals,

Jessica Schacht at the tasting bar. Photo: Centric Photography.

In the tasting room.
Photo: Marc Phillips.

including juniper, grains of paradise, orrisroot, coriander, cardamom, angelica, and calamus. The eighth ingredient is fresh lemon peel. "We use 150 fresh organic lemons and peel them by hand with a potato peeler," Ramona says. "Then all that fresh peel is infused into the gin." The alcohol by volume is 43.8 percent.

Nocino green walnut liqueur is a novel product that uses Cowichan Valley–grown green walnuts in a recipe developed by the team. Collecting the walnuts is a yearly affair that starts in distiller Alex's backyard, where the majority of the green walnuts grow. What are green walnuts? They are nuts that have not yet reached maturity and are harvested for a short time in the late spring. In their shell, green walnuts resemble small limes. Their undeveloped flesh is encased in a fragrant gelatine-like goo. Ampersand soaks them in vodka for several weeks, then sweetens the immature walnuts with local honey and further infuses it with cinnamon and allspice.

The liqueur's invention is credited to the Picts in Britain about 2,000 years ago. The occupying Romans brought it to Celtic France, and it eventually migrated to Italy, hence its name Nocino, which is derived from *noce*, Italian for walnut. Alcohol by volume is 27.1 percent.

Ampersand has teamed with Rathjen Cellars—which grows the grapes—to create Imperative Dry Vermouth, an herb-infused fortified wine to partner with its gin. It includes wormwood grown on the farm. They recommend mixing a martini with half Ampersand Gin and half Imperative Dry Vermouth.

In March 2020, the BC government authorized distilleries to begin producing hand sanitizer during the COVID-19 pandemic. Ampersand switched part of its production from spirits to hand sanitizer. Calling it "alcohol-based hand rub," it followed the World Health Organization's formula and included the tag line "For use between handwashing."

AWARDS

Ampersand has submitted its spirits to many competitions. "Winning competitions brings awareness to potential clients," says Ramona. "We get on people's radar when they're out buying spirits."

Ampersand Gin won a gold medal at the 2020 World Gin Awards, as well as gold medals with distinction at the 2019 and 2020 Canadian Artisan Spirit Competition. In 2016, 2017, and 2018, it was voted BC's Best Gin at the BC Distilled festival.

Per Se Vodka was named World's Best Varietal Vodka at the 2020 World Vodka Awards, while it also won a gold medal with distinction at the 2019 Canadian Artisan Spirit Competition. For the years 2016, 2017, 2018, and 2019, it was chosen by BC Distilled as BC's Best Vodka.

The distillery's Nocino green walnut liqueur nabbed a gold medal with distinction at the 2020 Canadian Artisan Spirit Competition and also collected double gold in the Non-Fruit Liqueur category at Sip Northwest's 2019 Best of the Northwest competition. Even its Imperative Dry Vermouth secured a bronze medal at the 2019 Canadian Artisan Spirit Competition.

TOURS

Ampersand offers tours by appointment. Check the website for any special events. The distillery participates in BC Distilled, the West Coast Grill Sooke Food & Brew Festival, and other craft spirit events. It can also be found at the Duncan Farmers' Market every Saturday and at the Oak Bay night market.

FAVOURITE COCKTAILS

NOCINO NEGRONI

1 oz (30 mL) Ampersand Gin
1 oz (30 mL) Nocino
1 oz (30 mL) Campari
Orange peel

Combine the ingredients in a rocks glass filled
with ice and stir. Garnish with orange peel.

A FIG AND GIN BEAUTY

½ oz (15 mL) Ampersand Gin
½ oz (15 mL) fig and vanilla simple syrup*
2 dashes orange bitters
1 oz (30 mL) Rootside Soda Cardamom Citrus Tonic
3 oz (90 mL) soda water
Figs for garnish

Shake the first three ingredients with ice. Strain into an ice-filled glass and top with the sodas. Garnish with figs.

*To make the fig and vanilla simple syrup, combine 6 fresh figs (halved, stems removed), ½ cup sugar, ½ cup water, and 1 vanilla bean (split and scraped) in a saucepan and bring to a boil. Reduce heat to medium and stir constantly for several minutes until figs break down. Remove from heat. Cool and strain. Store in refrigerator for up to 1 week.

SALT SPRING ISLAND

12
SALT SPRING SHINE CRAFT DISTILLERY

MICHAEL PAPP AND RIE OTSUBO-PAPP, CO-OWNERS

194 KITCHEN ROAD

SALT SPRING ISLAND, BC V8K 2B3

250-221-0728

MICHAEL@SALTSPRINGSHINE.COM

SALTSPRINGSHINE.COM

LATITUDE 48.807050, LONGITUDE -123.469623

MY DECEMBER VISIT TO SALT SPRING ISLAND TOOK
place on a rainy, misty day with low-hanging ragged cloud
obscuring the coastal mountain crests. Yet no matter the weather,
visiting this largest of the Gulf Islands is enjoyable for its peaceful
landscape, farms, meadows, and surrounding waters. The heavy
rain reminded me that coastal trees need plentiful moisture to
reach their great heights. After exiting the ferry, I drove along the
slaloming Fulford-Ganges Road toward Salt Spring Shine Craft
Distillery, delighted by the many roadside signs—free-range eggs,
pottery, wine, and a company advertising "Bark, compost and soil
blown anywhere you want."

It's a do-it-yourself entrepreneurial place, and Michael
Papp and Rie Otsubo-Papp fit
right in. Their Shine distillery is
built in the same style as their
house across the lawn, where
they live with their sons, Aidan
and Keegan. Michael built both
buildings using the property's
trees as much as possible. I ask
him if he's a construction guy;
he's quick to refute the idea.
"Just handy," he says. Early in
his life, he trained in tool and
die making. He says he learned
much about building from the
internet.

Michael, a lanky fellow,
arrived in 2010 at the heavily
treed property. Some of the
neatly cut logs are still stacked

Rie Otsubo-Papp and Michael
Papp at their tasting room
entrance.

next to the parking area. Michael built the house first while also taking a manager position at Garry Oaks Estate Winery.

Rie grew up in Fukuyama, Japan. As a teen, she accompanied her mother on an antique-buying trip to the UK—her mum sold British antiques—and the voyage inspired her to move to London to improve her English. After a year of studying the language, she wasn't yet ready to return to Japan, so she attended a finishing school. Then, as she enjoyed cooking, she enrolled at Le Cordon Bleu London. That's where she met Ontarian Michael Papp, who'd already completed his own studies at Le Cordon Bleu Ottawa Culinary Arts Institute, Canada's only Cordon Blue campus. He'd signed up for a few additional courses in England. After Rie completed her course, finding a rewarding job wasn't easy. She worked at several restaurants for long hours and low pay, finally opting to return home to Japan. Michael went back to Ontario. Their friendship endured through snail-mail letters and telephone calls, but long-distance romantic connections are difficult to maintain.

When they decided to make it permanent, Rie moved from Japan to Ontario, and the couple married in 1997. "We made that commitment to each other," says Rie, "and then opened a restaurant in Georgetown, about 45 minutes northwest of Toronto. It was located in a 100-year building, which we renovated. We called it the Simply Blue Bistro and served classic French cuisine, but it was influenced by Thai, Indian, and Japanese gastronomy as well."

Both worked in the restaurant, with Michael serving as chef and Rie handling the ordering and financial affairs. They lived in an apartment above the restaurant. The bistro was a success, but after their younger son, Keegan, was born, the long restaurant hours, six-day workweek, restricted family time and cramped space began to wear. "It was fun when we were younger," says Rie. "But we needed a lifestyle change after eight years in the restaurant." So they packed up the boys and went to Japan for two years. The rental income from the restaurant financed their stay there, while the pair also assisted Rie's parents in their respective antique and building businesses.

BUILDING THE DISTILLERY

Not wishing to return to Ontario, Michael and Rie scouted for a new place to live on the west coast. British Columbia was the place to be, they decided. They travelled around Vancouver Island, then took a look at Salt Spring Island. The slower pace and friendly lifestyle appealed, and the couple determined it would be the perfect location for them and their boys. Michael took a job as manager at the Garry Oaks Winery, increasing the knowledge about winemaking and fermentation that he'd already learned when doing a bit of hobby distilling.

When the BC craft distillery laws were enacted in 2013, they seized the opportunity and began working toward opening their own small-scale craft establishment. As with all alcohol licencing in BC, completing the paperwork took more than a year. But it was meeting the codes for building the distillery that was extremely demanding. "The code required a five-hour-rated firewall between the distilling room and the tasting room," says Michael. "It included multiple layers of drywall and two exits with steel doors."

They inaugurated Salt Spring Shine Craft Distillery in 2016. The spouses continue to work together while dividing responsibilities. Michael distills and maintains the property, and Rie manages the finances and fulfills the many reporting requirements of the BC Liquor and Cannabis Regulation Branch.

Michael is a self-taught distiller. "I learned a lot when I was manager at Garry Oaks," he says. "And distilling is not too difficult. It's an old established technology, not nuclear science. There's tons of information on the internet about distilling, equipment, yeast, and so on. I'd already done some amateur distilling with fruit in a pot still. And there's huge overlap

Michael Papp by his still.

between winemaking equipment and distillery equipment, like the fermenting tanks. So I'd acquired the background."

The tasting room's maple live-edge bar was hand cut by Michael. The matching shelves behind the bar support long lineups of their spirits. The combination looks artistic and pleasing—Michael obviously has skills beyond making spirits. An old-fashioned record player and a stack of vinyl 33s are ready to entertain visitors, or to inspire Michael when he's distilling.

The distillery displays several stainless steel fermenting tanks, the still, and the bottling/labelling station. It's an inviting, tidy space and even contains an oven for drying botanicals.

SHINE'S DISTILLING PROCESS

"We are presently the smallest distiller in the region," says Michael. "We might grow a bit more, but we have no intention of being one of the big ones."

That said, he runs his 200-litre Mile Hi still as much as he has time to. "Mile Hi is a Colorado company, and they make their stills in-house. They don't outsource their manufacturing to China. Its copper is solid. I can take the still apart, clean it, take out the plates. It's really adaptable. And the people at Mile Hi are easy to talk to when I have a question."

All the other stainless steel fermenting and storage tuns and tanks were fabricated in Pieve di Teco, a town in northwestern Italy, by Marchisio. The company started making carriages in 1898, but eventually switched to oenological and distilling equipment. Michael imported them for their quality and price.

Classic rock accompanies craft spirits.

A row of 375-millilitre bottles are awaiting their final gold-tinted top labels that will complete the Apple Pie Moonshine. The strips not only make the bottles look nifty but also demonstrate they haven't been tampered with.

The most important decision Michael and Rie made was to use honey as the base input for their spirits. The honey arrives in blue-painted metal barrels

Rie by the fermenting tanks.

from Golden Ears Apiaries, a beekeeping farm in Mission, BC. It's a much more expensive ingredient than a base derived from grains.

Michael says honey is the ingredient that gives Shine's vodka and gin their unique flavour and smoothness. He combines it with water from the natural well on their property, which, he says, is good-tasting water. The well water is untreated except for a UV light purifier that eliminates any unwanted organisms. While malted barley or fruit needs only a few days of fermenting, honey takes much longer, as it contains natural antibacterial ingredients that prevent quick fermentation. Michael ferments his honey for about seven to nine weeks.

The yeast he uses is a proprietary secret. "I believe in a low, slow ferment," he says. "I mix it manually." He shows me how he aerates the fermenting honey: an industrial-sized electric drill hangs over the edge of the fermenting tank and turns a drywall mud paddle. He also uses a winemaker trick called a pump-over or remontage, in which the honey from the bottom of the fermentation tank is brought up to the surface to release the carbon dioxide trapped in the lower part of the tank.

"I think fermentation is key to the final product," Michael says. "With honey, you have to watch the temperature and watch the process. The still does the same job no matter what you put into it. I believe there's too much emphasis on stills and not enough on fermentation. That's why I ferment our honey for such a long period and test it continually."

When the honey has fully fermented, he carries out a stripping run through the still—it removes water, yeast, and any sediment from the wash. There are no cuts, and the clear distillate leaving the still, also called low wine, is redistilled. It's during this redistillation that Michael uses his chef's training, years of cooking, and talented nose to cut the heads and tails from the hearts. "From a 200-litre run, I'll have a 10-litre head cut," he says. "That's a huge amount. I use the heads for cleaning equipment. The tails get redistilled with the next batch."

When asked what he'd tell other entrepreneurs wishing to enter the distilling craft, Michael responds, "You better like cleaning."

The distillery's products have been popular, and Michael and Rie are pleased with their success. Eventually, they'd like to add a whisky line. Michael has begun experimenting with honey-based whisky in 2- and 4-litre casks made of new Hungarian charred oak. He also plans to make limited batches of whisky for casks of 10 to 20 litres. For now, it's a question of time, storage space, and the cost of casks. As he says about constructing a home, a distillery, or planning for future expansion, "you build to the budget."

SHINE'S HONEY-INSPIRED SPIRITS

Honeycomb Moonshine is by far the strongest spirit Shine makes. It comes directly from the distilled hearts with its alcohol by volume reduced to 65 percent. "It has a bit of a kick," Michael warns, as he pours me a small taste. I drink only a tiny amount and the liquid explodes through my chest. Firewater indeed! I quickly quaff some water. Shine's Moonshine is likely a much purer version of the old homemade hooch once made secretly in the backwoods. It's not for the faint of heart drunk neat, but it's highly suitable for cocktails.

Hive Vodka is "reborn moonshine," Michael explains. It's proofed down with water to 50 percent alcohol by volume and then filtered once through activated charcoal. (According to Toronto's Sunnybrook Hospital website, "Activated charcoal is a black powder that may contain charred bone, coconut shells, peat, coal, olive pits, or even sawdust; it's more porous than regular charcoal.") Filtering through charcoal removes impurities from the spirit, impurities that could give vodka a bitter, harsh taste and smell. The slower the charcoal-filtering process, the cleaner and smoother the vodka. The final alcohol by volume is 40 percent.

Apple Pie Moonshine starts off with the moonshine base, then builds upon it with bins of mixed apples from Okanagan orchards. The apples are washed and chopped, then loaded into a fermenting tank with cinnamon, allspice, orange peel, and cloves. After three days, the wash is filtered. The result is a sweet, apple-scented liqueur without any added sugar. Its alcohol by volume is 30 percent. You can sip it neat or enjoy it on ice, with sparkling wine, in black tea, or over ice cream.

It's a hands-on job.

Sting Gin uses the filtered vodka base and transforms it into gin through the addition of 10 certified organic botanicals: juniper, coriander, angelica root, licorice, orange peel, lemon peel, lavender, rose petals, cardamom, and black pepper. These spices steep in the vodka, and then the two inputs are distilled together. The alcohol by volume is 40 percent.

The bottles for these four products are filled by hand, and the labels are also applied by hand. Sometimes the two sons pitch in with the labelling.

Shine joined other craft distilleries in producing hand sanitizer during the COVID-19 pandemic, after receiving temporary authorization to do so from the BC government. Shine called its product Hand Shine-Tizer.

AWARDS

In 2019, Salt Spring Shine Craft Distillery won silver medals for its Hive Vodka, Apple Pie Moonshine, and Sting Gin at the Canadian Artisan Spirit Competition hosted by Artisan Distillers Canada. Its Honeycomb Moonshine won a bronze medal.

13
SWEETWATER
DISTILLERY

DAVID AND FIONA WALLS, OWNERS

310 TOYNBEE ROAD

SALT SPRING ISLAND, BC V8K 2H7

250-801-8838

DAVID@SWEETWATERDISTILLERY.CA

SWEETWATERDISTILLERY.CA

LATITUDE 48.839678, LONGITUDE -123.528200

DAVID AND FIONA WALLS ARE CREATING A destination distillery on Salt Spring Island with a twofold mission. Their 40-acre property, Sweetwater Farm, has been part of the family since 1980; they are the second generation to operate it. The Wallses intend the distillery to be a family legacy enterprise that includes their three children—son Wesley Walls and daughters Jennifer Walls and Christina Haase—and their families.

"My father, Harry Walls, worked for Seagram's his whole life," David explains. "His wish was to build a winery on Salt Spring Island upon retirement. He and my mom, Joan Walls, bought the farm he named Sweetwater." The farm is aptly named, as it is known for the quality and taste of its delicious artesian spring water, an essential ingredient for their spirit production.

Neither David nor Fiona had retired yet when this book went into production. Fiona has a career in real estate on Salt Spring Island, while David has flown helicopters for decades. His piloting has taken him to Haiti in support of the United Nations' relief effort after the shattering 2010 earthquake there, and he's flown sorties on behalf of international oil exploration in such distant locations as Sudan and Mozambique. "I've been to 47 nations and airports," he says. "Many times

Sweetwater Distillery intends to be a multigenerational business.

I've only seen the airports." Closer to home, he helps fight forest fires in BC.

While the barn was being converted to house a 500-litre pot still, two 15-plate columns and a whisky helmet arrived from China through a Vancouver middleman company. "They're well made," says David, "with good welds." They will be installed as soon as all permits are in place and help is available.

The Wallses are also learning about the distilling process. Their first decision? Their base input for making spirits will be apples. "In the past, Salt Spring was the number one apple producer in British Columbia," says David, "well before the Okanagan became home to the prime orchards."

Sweetwater has 15 heritage apple trees on-site, and the Wallses will plant a five-acre orchard of apples suitable for their spirit input. In the meantime, they will secure apples from various British Columbia vendors and choose apple varieties based on their sugar content, or Brix. As Wikipedia explains, "Degrees Brix (symbol °Bx) is the sugar content of an aqueous solution. One degree Brix is 1 gram of sucrose in 100 grams of solution and represents the strength of the solution as percentage by mass. . . . The °Bx is traditionally used in the wine, sugar, carbonated beverage, fruit juice, maple syrup and honey industries." The sweetest apple varieties are Fuji, Honeycrisp, Ambrosia, Gala, Golden Delicious, and Red Delicious.

To learn first-hand about distilling, the Wallses have engaged expert Laurent Lafuente, a master-distiller consultant and a Swiss-trained French winemaker with vast experience in distilling and blending spirits. Laurent has assisted several distilleries get started and has also worked with other distilleries including Phillips Fermentorium and Merridale Cidery & Distillery.

The first products Sweetwater intends to produce are vodka and gin. Long-term goals include a rye-type whisky like Crown Royal.

If you plan to visit Salt Spring Island, or reside there, you have two distilleries to explore. You might combine this visit with a stop at Salt Spring's famous Saturday Market. Although Sweetwater Distillery's plan was to open in the summer of 2020, the COVID-19 pandemic slowed down the process, and the opening has been rescheduled for the spring of 2021. For information on visiting Sweetwater and its hours of operation, consult sweetwaterdistillery.ca.

NANAIMO REGION

14
ARBUTUS DISTILLERY

MIKE PIZZITELLI, OWNER AND DISTILLER

1890 BOXWOOD ROAD

NANAIMO, BC V9S 5Y2

250-714-0027

INFO@ARBUTUS-DISTILLERY.COM

ARBUTUSDISTILLERY.COM

LATITUDE 49.183587, LONGITUDE -123.985498

Mike Pizzitelli by his stills.
Photo: Marc Phillips.

BEFORE OPENING HIS SPACIOUS DISTILLERY AND cocktail lounge in Nanaimo, Mike Pizzitelli gained early experience with hobby beer brewing and spirit distilling in his hometown of Orillia, Ontario, a small city on Lake Simcoe, north of Toronto. "I always played around and experimented with alcohol," he says. This pastime likely influenced his choice to major in biochemistry at Western University, followed by a master's degree in cell biology. He believes his studies gave him a good base for distilling. "It honed my interests in strains of yeasts and nutrients," he says. "I also think distilling has similarities with a chef's culinary skills: the recipes, the tasting and judging of flavours."

To hone his distilling credentials, he enrolled for another master's degree at Heriot-Watt University in Edinburgh. The university's International Centre for Brewing and Distilling describes its master's program this way: "Research activities highlight qualities and molecular genetics of cereals, yeast and fermentation processes, beer and spirit stability and flavour." It's a year-long program that includes writing a thesis.

"For my thesis, I hunted wild yeasts that might have commercial value," Mike says. To locate these wild yeasts, he hiked around Edinburgh and found broken fermenting fruit, plant leaves, and flowers. "There's an endless supply of yeast," he says, "and we'd test to see if any of them could be ramped up for use in commercial brewing. Few are suitable, but you might hit on a good strain."

He returned home after his Scotland studies and found a job at the Flying Monkeys Craft Brewery in Barrie, Ontario. "Working there was good for them and me," he says. "I knew more about the science and theory of beer brewing, but they were more knowledgeable about the day-to-day operations, tools, and skills."

Mike Pizzitelli by the tasting bar.

His hands-on work included brewing, of course, but being in the brewery every day also taught him the importance of constant maintenance of equipment and machinery, and practical issues like packaging and freight.

"I had always a preference for distilling spirits," Mike continues. "But there were no craft distilleries, no job opportunities until the BC craft distillery laws changed in 2013." He applied for a licence right away. His savings and some family aid helped get him started. "No banks," he says. "I added equipment as funds allowed."

The distillery is located in a growing light-industrial area in the eastern section of Nanaimo, near Highway 19. "It's a good neighbourhood," says Mike. "There are enough businesses here that some coffee shops have opened."

The distillery was built from scratch, with room for the still, fermentation tanks, polybagged grains, bottling equipment, and cask storage. "I concentrated on the distillery first so I could start making spirits," says Mike. "And I built the tasting bar, but the cocktail lounge came later as it needed an additional licence."

The lounge is a pleasant area with tables crafted from thick wood slabs, flanked by solid wood stools on rollers. A rack fitted with grey linen fabric holds dried lemon balm and mint, along with other herbs hanging from the exposed plumbing—they may become part of a gin infusion or cocktail. The lounge is designed to entice patrons to linger. Board games like Scrabble, Clue, and Trivial Pursuit are stacked up, and a video game player/monitor is also available. One nook hosts comfortable leather chairs and a television. The back of the bar is lined with Arbutus's products, ready to be mixed or muddled into a cocktail or a flight.

Arbutus's cocktail lounge. Photo: Marc Phillips.

For a distillery to host a cocktail lounge, the law requires food to be available on the premises. Thus, next to the bar/lounge, a space has been carved out for a pizza oven and a prep area for appetizers. The cocktail lounge is open Thursday, Friday, and Saturday evenings, with two or three skilled bartenders ready to pour.

Asked if it was a lot of work to add food preparation to a distillery,

Arbutus's cocktail lounge.

Mike says he's sure having a bit of a kitchen, a cook, and servers is worth it because it so much enhances his spirits. "Just having a tasting bar doesn't make for a great experience," he says. "The small, cozy atmosphere of the lounge with a mix of appies and cocktails is so much better for actually tasting the spirits we make. Our bartenders are like chefs making enticing drinks. We play music, have games, have a bit of fun."

I ask Mike why he opted to construct a new building rather than retrofit an existing one. "Refitting is very expensive," he explains. "Just retrofitting an interior sprinkling system and other fire suppression equipment, as required by code, is very costly. Here, I could divide our space into public and private segments, have a bit of a kitchen, put in the plumbing and electricity we need from the beginning. I could buy the land. Zoning for distilleries is very tough. I could not have been permitted to construct this facility in Nanaimo's downtown."

Arbutus's big 1,000-litre still was manufactured by venerable German still maker Ulrich Kothe Destillationstechnik, located in Eislingen. Fermentation tanks reside next to the still, and polybags of special malt barley from Gambrinus Malting, based in Armstrong, BC, recline on pallets. Mike doesn't malt on-site, but a farmer near Nanaimo also delivers one-tonne bags with clean grain. "With my assistant, Will Oxland, we are working at capacity," he says. "We are distilling as much as we can."

During the summer, Mike grows many of his own herbs in wood boxes and planters around the distillery as well as on part of the flat roof. "We try to get organic seeds and do not use any chemicals on the herbs," he says.

Looking ahead, Mike has applied for a licence for a nano-brewery for beer drinkers frequenting the cocktail lounge and to promote growler sales.

He plans to use his depleted casks—those that no longer provide proper flavour to a spirit—to season the beer he will be brewing. "In my view," he says, "the first use of a cask leads to considerable drawing out of flavour. The second use still imparts much flavour to the spirit. By the third use, you may be depleting the flavour. At the end of a barrel's life, we can age beer in it, especially higher-proof beer of 11–12 percent."

Mike's fertile brain is always thinking up new products to add to his repertoire. He's brewing his own kombucha, a fermented tea flavoured with botanicals such as juniper and orange pekoe. Patrons can fill their kombucha growlers at the tasting bar.

Plans are afoot to buy a second, 3,000-litre still in 2020–21.

ARBUTUS'S PRODUCTS

For clear spirits, Mike uses mostly milled and malted barley, rye, and wheat, which ferment in their tanks to an alcohol content of about 11 percent. The wash is then double-distilled to reach alcohol content in the 90s. For his Empiric Gin, he redistills the ethanol a third time with the botanicals included.

Mike is laying up various whiskies, which will be released upon maturity. Besides single malt, three casks of 100 percent rye whisky are maturing for 2021 launch. They are stored in new oak casks or casks formerly filled with different types of alcohol.

Arbutus's signature gin.
Photo: Marc Phillips.

Arbutus's flagship spirits include Coven Vodka, Empiric Gin, and Baba Yaga Genuine Absinthe.

Coven Vodka is a rich, smooth, small-batch spirit copper-pot-distilled from 100 percent BC-grown and BC-malted barley. Arbutus uses European-style techniques that highlight the flavour characteristics of the grain. (Western-style vodkas are distilled and filtered to create a neutral spirit.) The alcohol by volume is 40 percent.

Empiric Gin has merged the company's vodka with classic botanicals like juniper and coriander, along with such coastal staples as hops, rosemary, anise hyssop (in the mint family), fennel, mint, and lavender. To create the gin's citrus tones, Arbutus adds lemon verbena instead of citrus peels and rinds. Mike calls it a "true west coast gin." The alcohol by volume is 40 percent.

The Empiric name and packaging are inspired by the medieval "death doctors," whose beaklike masks were stuffed with aromatic botanicals to reduce bad odours. They are also believed to have used juniper-based tinctures to ward off the plague.

Citrus Gin, launched at the end of 2019, resembles a London dry gin but uses somewhat different botanicals in the distilling process. Besides juniper, coriander, orrisroot, and angelica, Mike adds elderflower and four kinds of citrus—lemon peel, orange peel, dry salted limes, and kaffir lime leaves. The alcohol by volume is 43 percent.

Baba Yaga Genuine Absinthe has been distilled in the traditional method with grand wormwood, anise, fennel, lemon balm, and mint. Arbutus ages its absinthe in new, toasted or charred American oak casks. The finished spirit rests and steeps in more herbs and botanicals, creating a natural green-chartreuse colour. Over time, the green herbs may leave a natural green haze in their bottle. The spirit can be enjoyed over ice, paired with sparkling wine, or mixed in cocktails. The alcohol by volume is a colossal 60 percent. A favourite tipple of late 19th-century and early 20th-century artists, writers, and performers living in Paris, absinthe was famously imbibed by such painters as Manet, Degas, and Picasso.

Arbutus released its three-year Canadian Single Malt Whisky—about 500 bottles—in 2019. It sold out right away. The whisky was made from 100 percent BC-malted barley, distilled in the traditional copper pot and column still. Mike matured one part of the whisky for three years in casks that previously stored bourbon; the second version rebarrelled the bourbon-cask-aged whisky in new American oak barrels—thus extracting an additional flavour. Mike then blended the two whiskies, whose colour derives from the casks' interior wood, charring, and previous occupant. No caramel or artificial colouring was added. The alcohol by volume is 43 percent. Other whiskies are awaiting their birthday of three years and one day—or more.

In addition to its flagship spirits and whisky, Arbutus produces a series of small-batch flavoured gins and liqueurs. Sometimes they're sold out, or Mike has dreamt up a new flavour. But there are many to choose from, so if one of them isn't available, try another.

For Arbutus's Blue Gin, Mike starts with Empiric Gin and redistills it with the butterfly pea flower, an herbal tea blossom that originates in Southeast Asia. Its pigment transforms the spirit's clarity into a sapphire blue. The alcohol by volume is 40 percent.

Forest Dweller Gin or Coniferous Aged Gin begins with Empiric Gin that is then infused with a mix of spruce, pine, and grand fir needles. It makes for a piney, west coast gin. The alcohol by volume is 40 percent.

Vanilla Liqueur is made with organic vanilla beans that travel to Nanaimo from the Democratic Republic of the Congo. Mike macerates the vanilla beans and steeps them in vodka for a month in a stainless steel vat. The extracted vanilla-flavoured liqueur is sweetened with cane sugar. The alcohol by volume is 20 percent.

Owl's Screech Vodka can be a "weird concoction," says Mike, and may change from batch to batch. Limited to the summer season, it's flavoured with yams and cashews and then hotted up with Scotch bonnets and jalapeños grown by the Vancouver Island Hot Sauce Company in Nanoose Bay. It's perfect for those who like their Caesars spicy or super spicy, or those who like the "contrast of heat over ice." The alcohol by volume is 35 percent.

Elderflower Liqueur, as the name implies, is vodka infused with foraged and cultivated elderflower blossoms. "We make it in the late spring when the flowers are at their peak," says Mike. "Local pickers bring us the goods." The alcohol by volume is 22 percent.

Crème de Lavande or Lavender Liqueur again starts with clear ethanol and is infused with freshly gathered Vancouver Island lavender. The alcohol by volume is 20 percent.

Limoncello Liqueur may hark back to Mike's Italian heritage, as limoncello is the second most popular liqueur in Italy.

It's made from Arbutus vodka with added lemon peel, lemon juice, and sugar. The alcohol by volume is 28 percent.

Birch Liqueur is made with syrup tapped from British Columbia birch trees in the early spring when tree sap begins moving. Gatherers tap the trees and bring the sap to a sugar shack to make syrup. "Birch syrup has a taste similar to molasses," says Mike. The alcohol by volume is 25 percent.

Amaro Bitter Liqueur is an experimental drink. "We use bittering herbs," says Mike. "I find free-range herbs. There are endless possibilities, and this liqueur will vary. The alcohol by volume is 30 percent.

Along with other craft distillers, Arbutus added hand sanitizer to its production of spirits during the COVID-19 pandemic. Mike emphasized that his sanitizer was "not for human consumption" because it contained hydrogen peroxide as well as 75 percent alcohol, glycerine, aloe vera, essential oils, botanicals, and food colouring.

AWARDS

Mike began entering his spirits in competitions in 2018 and has earned a bevy of medals. He has preferred entering his products in Canadian contests.

Among his spirits, Baba Yaga absinthe won gold and best in class, and Forest Dweller Gin was awarded gold with a distinction for Excellence in Terroir at the 2020 Canadian Artisan Spirit Competition. Crème de Lavande, Citrus Gin, and Coven Vodka won silver medals at the same competition.

At the 2019 Canadian Artisan Spirit Competition, Baba Yaga won gold while Empiric Gin and Mike's first single malt whisky were recognized with silver medals.

FAVOURITE COCKTAIL

OLD FASHIONED COCKTAIL

Sugar cube
Cocktail bitters
1½ oz (45 mL) double-barrelled whisky
Orange peel
Cherry

Place the sugar cube in the bottom of a glass and pour the bitters on top. Stir well. Add one to two ice cubes and the whisky. Stir two or three times to chill, then garnish with orange peel and cherry.

15
BESPOKE
SPIRITS HOUSE

SHELLY HEPPNER, OWNER AND DISTILLER

105–425 STANFORD AVENUE EAST

PARKSVILLE, BC V9P 2N4

250-228-5385

HELLO@BESPOKESPIRITSHOUSE.COM

BESPOKESPIRITSHOUSE.COM

LATITUDE 49.316213, LONGITUDE -124.299053

WITH THE TAG LINE "PART ART, PART SCIENCE—
unadulterated enjoyment!" Shelly Heppner launched her distillery, Bespoke Spirits House, in the summer of 2020, becoming one of the most recent spirit producers on Vancouver Island.

Although she'd completed the paperwork requirements for opening her enterprise, she was still awaiting liquor branch approval of her bottle labels. I ask her if the BC government has to approve labels. "Indeed, they do," she responds. "There are several regulations. Labels must display standard information on what type of spirit is inside the bottle and the alcohol-by-volume content. And labels cannot promote the blatant use of alcohol and must avoid raunchy language."

Shelly's background includes several careers, working in retail and with large corporations like TELUS, with her work focusing on customer service. In her spare time, she concentrated on artistic enterprises, becoming a self-taught artist. She made glass mosaics and reinvented worn furniture with gold leafing and decoupage. She also facilitated continuing education classes on mosaic making at Vancouver and Burnaby schools.

"I have an inherent need to express my creativity," says Shelly, who calls herself Parksville's Spirit Mistress. "I was always stifled in the mainstream workforce. What I excelled at in that world was using my problem-solving skills. So I'm an enigma—a highly creative, analytical individual."

For Shelly, initiating a distillery was an avenue toward exploring her creative side more intensely. "I found the idea of making gin fascinating," she explains. "My creative canvas changed to a liquid process. I began researching the distilling process and its history. Then I studied the requirements I needed to fulfill to open a distillery."

Shelly Heppner by her still.
Courtesy Bespoke.

Shelly knew she needed to gain the technical and business knowledge of running a distillery. So she signed up for the Urban Distilleries Master Distiller Workshop in Kelowna and also attended workshops offered during the American Distilling Institute conference ("The Voice of Craft Distilling") in Portland, Oregon. A week-long workshop at Sons of Vancouver Distillery's Distiller School on distilling techniques further honed her spirit-making skills.

She feels lucky to have snagged a lease space in a commercial development in downtown Parksville. "It was zoned right to start with," she says. "It came with 18-foot ceilings, and it's a great location. The City of Parksville was very supportive." She obtained all the licences she needed in about 16 months—a relatively short time for opening a distillery from scratch.

Shelly found her distilling equipment in Wenzhou, China, an industrial city with more than nine million inhabitants. She had been reassured by the distilling community that the equipment was proven. "I emailed back and forth with this industrial company for six months, deciding what I wanted and needed," she recalls.

In early 2020, her polished, stainless steel, all-jacketed order arrived: two 1,000-litre fermenters; a 1,000-litre mash/stripping still; a 500-litre, 12-plate column still; a 250-litre gin still; and a blending motor. The electrical systems were certified. She also obtained a natural gas–fuelled steam boiler, unique in that it's a contained unit with no open flame—the first BC distillery to install this type of system.

Using winter wheat from South Peace Grain in Dawson Creek, BC, she plans to distill neutral spirits, create a vodka called Virtue, and then focus on gin production. She's developing her first gin, called Jezebel, and choosing the botanicals.

Shelly Heppner by her pot still. Courtesy Bespoke.

Once her distillery is operating at full tilt, she also wants to create seasonal, limited-release spirits, including fruit-based eaux-de-vie, liqueurs, and custom runs for individuals or companies. She's also dreamed up an innovative concept she calls "gin sensory workshops." She will extract the essence from botanicals such as juniper, coriander, and angelica, then invite small groups to add these essences, drop by drop, into their gin. This way tasters can create their own, personalized version of gin and order bottles for themselves or as gifts for friends, weddings, and so forth.

By the time this book went to press, Shelly was in the very early stages of distilling. But Parksville is a good place to visit on your distillery tour, and she invites you to stop by to sample her elixirs. Her website lists the times she is open.

16
MISGUIDED SPIRITS CRAFT DISTILLERY

DARRELL BELLAART, OWNER AND DISTILLER

18-1343 ALBERNI HIGHWAY

PARKSVILLE, BC V9P 2B9

250-586-2200

DARRELL@MISGUIDEDSPIRITS.CA

MISGUIDEDSPIRITS.CA

LATITUDE 49.306534, LONGITUDE -124.355733

MISGUIDED SPIRITS OPENED ITS DOORS IN EARLY 2020, with the owner, Darrell Bellaart, switching from a journalism career to one off the beaten track—distilling spirits. I thought perhaps that led to the unusual moniker for his spirit house.

But Darrell put me straight. "When my wife, Deirdre, and I began talking about a distillery name, we thought Ocean Spirits would reflect our Vancouver Island location surrounded by salt water." Alas, a search of registered trade names revealed that three companies had already laid claim to that name.

The couple was disappointed and kept searching for a new name. But one day, after Deirdre used the term *misguided* in a sentence, a light went off. "How about Misguided Spirits?" Darrell joked. They looked at each other and Misguided was born.

While we're explaining word choices, the distillery's vodka is called Brother XII. That name reveals the history of a Vancouver Island cult leader, Edward Arthur Wilson, an English-born mystic, swindler, and scammer. He's been compared to such later quasi-religious leaders as Jim Jones and David Koresh. Renamed Brother XII, he led a small group of well-off people to a commune-like setting near Nanaimo and several Gulf Islands. As is often the case with charismatic leaders, the interplay of power, money, and sex came to dominate the cult and engendered sensational headlines in the 1920s. Eventually, disgruntled followers threatened a

Misguided Spirits' vodka label. Courtesy Deirdre Bellaart.

Misguided's tasting room. Photo: Deirdre Bellaart.

lawsuit, and Brother XII disappeared with a reported fortune in gold. Misguided's vodka label, designed by the Nanaimo-based creative firm Primal Communications, features a bearded Brother XII seemingly surrounded by hellfire.

Darrell was one of the casualties of the shrinking newspaper business. After reporting for various newspapers and ending at the *Nanaimo Daily News*, he was laid off in 2016 when the newspaper ceased publication.

"As I'd had a long interest in alcohol production, Deirdre encouraged me to look into distilling as a next career," says Darrell. He'd already had decades of experience in brewing, winemaking and home distilling. As a child, along with his two older brothers, he received a chemistry set for Christmas, and when he was just 10, he built a little still (with his dad's help, he confesses) for the annual Edmonton Regional Science Fair. "I distilled water," he says, "and put some food colouring in the wash. It came out clear."

He also had a yen to try fermentation. "I put grapes, sugar, and yeast in a glass jar and hid it in the closet. It blew up." As an adult, after he bought his first house in 1992, he began winemaking. But home distilling murmured in the back of his mind. "I spent time reading alcohol-making treatises on the internet so I wouldn't poison us. After I bought a 30-litre still from Broken Oar Distilling Equipment, I made vodka and rum for my wife and our friends."

FINDING A LOCATION

It's tough to find a building capable of housing a distillery. As the craft distilling industry is young, some regions and municipalities aren't yet familiar with its potential and remain wary of potential fire and explosion dangers—perhaps some remember their own experiments with grapes and yeast in the closet. That said, alcohol vapour can ignite, and fire prevention must be part of a distillery's plan. Darrell did eventually find a 1,500-square-foot spot in a light-industrial area and began paying rent in 2018. It's near Coombs and close to the Old Country Market, well known for its restaurant with goats on the roof.

He developed a detailed business plan with the help of WorkBC, which offers a self-employment course. "They give great assistance and deserve much credit for what they do," he says. He submitted drawings of the distillery to the Regional District of Nanaimo's planning department and fulfilled zoning and licensing requisites. Electrical hookups became a headache. "Every time I turned around there was another regulation," he recalls. "New three-phase electrical wiring, new panel. I spent twice what I'd anticipated."

But, by January 2020, he'd conquered the obstacles and formally opened Misguided Spirits. While awaiting the proper

Darrell Bellaart distilling. Photo: Deirdre Bellaart.

permits and preparing for his start-up, he'd built a good-looking bar in a well-appointed tasting room and installed his equipment in the distilling area. He'd enrolled in a week-long, hands-on distilling program with the Distillery School, run by James Lester and Richard Klaus's Sons of Vancouver Distillery. And he'd also bought a 1,000-litre, square, stainless steel stripping pot still from Sons of Vancouver, which had obtained it from the 2bar Spirits distillery in Seattle.

Darrell modified the stripping still, replacing the single-phase elements with three-phase, low-watt density elements to improve efficiency and reduce the risk of scorching the low wines. He also acquired a second, 400-litre, eight-plate pot still with a 15-centimetre column manufactured by the Wenzhou Yayi Light Industrial Machinery Company, located in China.

THE DISTILLING PROCESS

Darrell chose as his base input 70 percent wheat from South Peace Grain and 30 percent malted barley from Phillips in Victoria. The wheat comes already cracked. Darrell told me in detail how he approaches his distilling progression.

He mashes his grain in a 1,500-litre dairy tank, which also originated with 2bar Spirits in Seattle. 2bar converted the dairy tank to a mash tun by installing a false bottom to accommodate traditional brewhouse-style sparge mashing. While filling the tank to the 300-litre line with 82°C (180°F) water, Darrell rushes to mill three 25-kilogram bags of malted barley, which are dumped along with seven bags of distillers wheat into the mash. He stirs hard to mix the grain with the hot water, which begins the starch conversion. "That combination is the sweet spot," he says. "The barley adds the enzymes and interesting notes of barley flavour."

He cooks the mixture for about three hours, while a motorized stirring device churns the mash. After resting the mash for about 30 minutes, he drains the wort (the sugary water) into a 1,000-litre plastic storage tote, then fills the mash tank twice more with water in a sparging process—a practice that's designed to rinse every last bit of the remaining sugars out of the mash. "When I've completed the third sparge, I only have the spent grain left in the mash tun," he says. "That goes to farmers as animal food."

The following day, he pitches the yeast into the storage tote, and then he ferments the resulting wash for up to seven days. His stripping run delivers a low wine of 30 percent. His final spirit distillation run produces at least 90 percent pure alcohol—which is cut to 40 percent alcohol by volume in his Brother XII vodka.

He filters his vodka twice through activated charcoal to attain its crystal-clear look. He says visitors who have tasted his vodka praise its smooth vanilla and caramel flavours.

Misguided's marketing has focused on private liquor stores, and on Facebook and Instagram. In March 2020, after the BC government authorized distilleries to produce hand sanitizer during the

Working on the still.
Photo: Deirdre Bellaart.

COVID-19 pandemic, Misguided joined other craft distillers by adding hand sanitizer to its spirit production.

At the time I spoke with Darrell, he was working on the recipe for his next spirit—gin. Also on the horizon was the development of several liqueurs.

As with all small-business start-ups, there are hoops to jump through and challenges to overcome. Asked if it's worth the hassles, Darrel answers without equivocation: "Working alone in the distillery is a delight. I love being my own boss. I'm lucky doing what I love to do."

TOURS

For a tour and tasting schedule, consult the website.

FAVOURITE COCKTAIL

MOSCOW MULE

1½ oz (45 mL) Misguided Spirits Brother XII
    Vodka

Rootside Soda Ginger Beer

Squeeze of lime

Lime wedge

Pour on ice and garnish with a lime wedge.

WEST COAST
VANCOUVER
ISLAND

17
TOFINO
DISTILLERY

ADAM WARRY, JOHN GILMOUR, AND NEIL CAMPBELL
    CO-OWNERS

681 INDUSTRIAL WAY, UNITS G AND H

BOX 479

TOFINO, BC V0R 2Z0

250-725-2182

INFO@TOFINOCRAFTDISTILLERY.COM

TOFINOCRAFTDISTILLERY.COM

LATITUDE 49.1396, LONGITUDE -125.8918

Why people visit Tofino.

TO REACH THE TOFINO AND PACIFIC RIM DISTILLERIES

takes some persistence—although it's worth it. Driving from Highway 19 and taking Route 4 west, you must traverse about 165 kilometres of tortuous road twisting among mountains and along lakes, creeks, and the Alberni Inlet. In clear weather, the natural landscapes are awe inspiring. I was stopped twice because the road seems to be under permanent construction. The wait was about an hour, giving me a chance to stretch my legs, listen to rushing water in an invisible creek, look at the salal bushes growing new leaves in February, and socialize with a truck driver transporting fresh seafood who took advantage of lost time to clean his windshield.

Travelling this slow road is a good introduction to Vancouver Island's laid-back, most westerly shores, where the Pacific Rim National Park Reserve displays its stupendous beaches. It's a surfers' nirvana. Several waterfronts are filled with black-clad surfboarders hoping to stay upright in the roaring surge. They surf year-round, even in winter's cold temperatures.

Tofino started as an isolated fishing town, then became a haven for hippies once a road connected the region to the rest of Vancouver Island. Most of the hippies are gone now, but the area remains full of people who search out locally grown and prepared food and drink, who pluck plastic from the beaches and care deeply about environmental sustainability.

The three owners of Tofino Distillery, Adam Warry, 42, John Gilmour, 36, and Neil Campbell, 34, fit perfectly in this environment. They have chosen to use only organic ingredients to produce their spirits and have obtained organic certification. "We like the idea of higher-quality farming," says Adam. "And we have a passion for craft." In their eyes, *organic*, or grains and botanicals grown without agricultural chemicals, means that their products are traditional and authentic.

Neil delivers their products in a Prius, and plans are afoot to acquire a Tesla to reduce emissions to zero. They've decided to forgo social media, focusing instead on producing spirits "without the bombardment from Facebook, Twitter, and so on," Neil tells me. "We also wanted to create an intimate atmosphere at the distillery. We like the more traditional way of doing things. Although it's tough sometimes to get people off their phones while tasting cocktails."

The owners simply named their distillery Tofino. "We are based here and are proud of our small community's character," says Neil. They also added nautical motifs to their labels—an old-fashioned diving helmet and a compass rose—harking back to the town's earlier maritime character.

The three owners all serve as volunteer firemen in Tofino—with John being a former chief—so they have past experience collaborating as a team. Adam also worked as a paramedic. Neil, who has a political science degree from Ottawa's Carleton

Tofino Distillery's head distiller, Adam Warry.

Tofino Distillery in its light-industrial bay.

University, moved across Canada directly to the west coast. "I was looking for something more about 12 years ago, and a friend told me he had a room available in Tofino," Neil says. "I came and never left. Most recently, I worked at the Tofino Brewing Company for four years."

John had lived in an off-the-grid floathouse near Meares Island and had plans to develop a biofuel enterprise using Jerusalem artichokes with their high sugar content. "My experimentation was a precursor to making spirits," he says. "I had a small four-acre farm and planted artichokes. Unfortunately, it didn't work—much more land is needed. My next logical step was home brewing and vodka distilling, just to see if it was viable. Adam and I teamed up in 2016."

Adam has been a plumber and an electrician and says that he's spent a lifetime learning. "I also made wine and beer as a hobby," he adds. "I learned by trial and error. Did a lot of research on the internet and read books. The distillery has allowed me to scale up from 10 to 500 litres."

To obtain the required licences, find a zoned and licensed workspace, and arrange financing took about a year. In the

Tofino's cocktail lounge and tasting bar.

meantime, John and Adam attended the Kelowna-based Urban Distilleries Master Distiller Workshop. They leased a bay in a light-industrial area that also houses the Summit Bread Company. The bay came with its steel studs exposed; municipal regulations demanded the installation of a double layer of fire-rated drywall over the studs. Tofino Distillery opened formally in 2018.

The spacious quarters house the distilling area, with its stills, fermenting tanks, and grain storage. The tasting bar and lounge share a space to welcome visitors. Cable-spool tables with wooden bar stools invite the slow sipping of a cocktail. Live plants are scattered around. The bar features shelves with Tofino's spirits and a large mirror, which makes the space seem larger.

A series of 24 casks, containing bourbon, rye, and single malt whiskies, are maturing on sturdy racks that separate the public space from the distillery, setting up a barrier but still allowing

John Gilmour explains the distilling process.

tipplers to get glimpses of the distilling process. The whisky is slated to age for five years, although an earlier release might take place in the fall of 2021. "It might be okay to release some then," says Adam. "But we might keep maturing our spirits longer to make sure they're really optimum."

Working as a trio, the partners have each established their own "sphere of influence" so their tasks don't overlap. John explains that a business partnership "is like a marriage, where you have to work things out. We've been good friends who have held together through our growing pains." All three participate in spirit production, but Adam is the head distiller aided by the other two whenever needed. John, who has the most business experience, handles business development, payroll, and reporting to the government on every aspect of alcohol production—a time-consuming task. Neil markets and distributes Tofino's spirits to more than 300 customers on both Vancouver Island and the mainland, thus spending much time on the road. They all take turns tending the tasting bar.

To get their distillery off the ground financially, they developed a detailed business plan. John says it takes a fair amount to get started. "The three of us invested," says John, "but smaller banks were also interested in loaning money. By the time we applied, roughly four years after the BC laws allowed craft distilleries to open up, it had become a proven business model. And other people also wanted to invest."

THE DISTILLING PROCESS

The troika bought two Genio stills manufactured in Poland. The 500-litre pot still is dedicated to stripping runs, while the 250-litre still takes the alcohol to its 95 percent purity level. "The Genio customer service was excellent," says John. "Guys came from Poland to set it up. And although we know how to fix equipment, they came out three times to make sure the stills worked perfectly." The stills contain a clean-in-place spray system, which removes sulphuric compounds that build up after several batches of wash are distilled. One still displays part of a column packed with copper coils. According to the Genio website, this design uses "Spiral Prismatic Packing," which allows the manufacturer to "minimize the size of the still, reducing operating costs, while obtaining the maximum amount of distillate."

Part of a column packed with copper coils that remove impurities.

When I visited the distillery, a 2,000-litre still fabricated by Victoria-based Specific Mechanical Systems was on order. "This still has been designed for us and will be a hybrid, multi-purpose still," says Adam.

Along one side of the bay, large polyvinyl bags of rye, corn, and wheat rest on wall racks. Below them, rolls of printed spirit labels hang on a rod, ready to be applied. Tofino Distillery is a hands-on enterprise.

Individual yeasts, essential fermentation ingredients, are chosen for each spirit. The distillery buys its corn, rye, and barley in 1,000-kilogram sacks from Fieldstone Organics, based in Armstrong, BC. "It's our own mix, and we make a traditional bourbon-style whisky with it," says Adam. Rye is the base for their Canadian-style whisky. To produce their vodka and gin, the Tofino team uses soft winter wheat.

"We buy our botanicals from a private company to make sure we get only certified organic botanicals and thus maintain our own organic certification," says Neil.

Their whiskies are stored in new American oak barrels that have been charred from medium to heavy, "alligator skin" levels. They're supplied by Seguin Moreau, a French cask fabricator that maintains a cooperage in Napa, California. Tofino's goal is to produce 100 barrels of the various whiskies per year, allow them to age gracefully, and bottle them at their peak flavour.

Spent grain—the residues of the distilling process—goes to Cedar, BC, where it feeds livestock. The spent botanicals are composted.

TOFINO DISTILLERY'S PRODUCTS

Tofino's vodka is produced in the 250-litre still in small batches, using certified organic winter wheat as its base. Adam says that the way the distillery filters this vodka makes for a 95 percent clean and smooth product. He also cites the distillery's use of pristine Tofino water, which is piped from rainwater reservoirs on nearby Meares Island. The reservoirs are fed by abundant west coast rainwater filtered through the surrounding watershed. Alcohol by volume is 40 percent.

Jalapeño Vodka incorporates jalapeño hot peppers grown in BC during the summer and in Mexico during the winter. The peppers are macerated and infuse the vodka in a stainless steel vat for five to seven days. The length of the infusion depends on the jalapeño's heat, as it can vary from season to season. You can mix it with mango juice and a splash of lime or create an extra-spicy Caesar. Alcohol by volume is 40 percent.

To create their Espresso Vodka, the distillers teamed up with Creekmore's Coffee, a small-batch, certified organic, fair-trade, wholesale roaster in Coombs, BC. The dark roasted coffee beans and grounds are packed into a silk bag and infused in Tofino's vodka for at least a week. No sugar is added to this flavoured vodka. Its recommended use is in traditional coffees, cocktail shafts, and White Russians. You can even quaff your caffeine in an espresso martini. Alcohol by volume is 40 percent.

West Coast Gin, as the name implies, is based on a traditional recipe that incorporates west coast flavours. Gin has ancient roots. It was in the 14th century that gin was crafted in the Netherlands as a medicinal tonic. The spirit is called jenever or genever. Over the centuries, it was widely exported, and it became popular in the UK after Dutch-born William of Orange became king in the 1700s. Tofino's gin is flavoured with 10 botanicals: juniper, coriander, angelica root, orrisroot, lemon peel, orange peel, grains of paradise, cardamom, licorice root, and cubeb berries. The juniper is imported from Croatia. (The countries that formerly made up Yugoslavia are major exporters of juniper berries.)

Tofino's gin is non-chill filtered, which, according to Adam, retains flavour. But, as Tofino Distillery explains on its website, "Don't be alarmed if a little Tofino fog rolls into your glass when adding ice or putting your bottle in the fridge. It becomes cloudy at 0°C." Alcohol by volume is 45 percent.

Rose Hibiscus Gin begins its life as West Coast Gin, but the botanicals are added in different ratios, and the additions of rosebuds and hibiscus flowers deliver its deep pink colour, along with its distinct rose flavour and hints of hibiscus. Alcohol by volume is 45 percent.

One of Tofino's West Coast gins.

Old Growth Cedar Gin is again infused with the same botanicals as West Coast Gin, with one major addition: the gin basket is stuffed with western red cedar tips. The tips are picked in the spring and dried so they can be used the entire year. This one botanical addition changes the flavour and texture of the gin significantly.

The Tofino distillers say that the addition of cedar flavour to this small-batch gin truly reflects the coastal, temperate, old-growth rainforest of western Canada. Alcohol by volume is 45 percent.

Psychedelic Jellyfish Absinthe is made with large amounts of wormwood, anise, fennel, hyssop, and lemon balm. It exhibits heavy notes of anise and is tinted with the green colour of maple leaves. The distillers really pushed the limits with this spirit: it contains 73 percent alcohol by volume (146 proof). To drink this absinthe, it must be diluted—or it could burn your taste buds. The French drink the spirit by dripping ice-cold water over a sugar cube placed on a slotted spoon over a glass of absinthe.

On their website, the distillers salute the Green Fairy—a translation of *la fée verte*—a French nickname that became interchangeable with absinthe. It was used to describe the favourite drink of poets, painters, and other artists at the end of the 19th and early 20th centuries. Absinthe was believed to inspire creativity. Some have called it the "cocaine of the 19th century." Such luminaries as Ernest Hemingway, Pablo Picasso, Vincent van Gogh, Oscar Wilde, Marcel Proust, Erik Satie, and Edgar Allan Poe were known imbibers. One of absinthe's botanicals, thujone (present in wormwood), was considered so hallucinogenic that absinthe was banned for a century in many Western countries. More recently, thujone has been found to be no more dangerous than alcohol in general. British Columbia does not regulate wormwood content but does require absinthe to be lab tested to assess thujone content before production and sale.

Tofino's Beach Fire flavours its vodka with peppery cinnamon. "We want to capture the idea of a communal spirit around the campfire," says John. Alcohol by volume is 30 percent.

Two liqueurs, Limoncello and Lavender Mint Gin, are available seasonally. "Our bartender, Kat Thomas, peels fresh organic lemons," says Neil, "and their juice and peel is infused into our vodka along with sugar. It has a beautiful yellow colour."

The Lavender Mint Gin is made the same way, with organic lavender and mint infused into Tofino's West Coast Gin. The alcohol by volume for both liqueurs is 35 percent.

In the spring of 2020, Tofino Distillery contributed its ethanol hearts to the production of hand sanitizer. Its formula included 75 percent alcohol, some glycerine, and a healthy dose of hydrogen peroxide. They've been making the sanitizer for first responders, hospitals, and clinics in the west coast Vancouver Island region.

AWARDS AND INFORMATION

Tofino Distillery has not applied for any awards. Information on the tasting room and open hours can be found on the website.

When you wish to visit Tofino and Ucluelet, check for road closings or delays at drivebc.ca/mobile/pub/events/Highway4 .html.

FAVOURITE COCKTAILS

THE BEE'S KNEES

2 oz (60 mL) Rose Hibiscus Gin

1 oz (30 mL) fresh lemon juice

¾ oz (22 mL) honey syrup (1:1 honey and hot water)

3 oz (90 mL) soda water

Lemon slices

Rose petals

Shake the Rose Hibiscus Gin, lemon juice, and honey syrup over ice. Strain into a Collins glass over ice. Top with the soda. Garnish with lemon slices and rose petals.

TIPTOE THROUGH THE TULIPS

¾ oz (22 mL) Psychedelic Jellyfish Absinthe

½ oz (15 mL) fresh lemon juice

½ oz (15 mL) lavender syrup*

3 oz (90 mL) water

Combine all ingredients, mix well, and serve over ice in a Collins glass.

*To make the lavender syrup, bring 2 cups sugar, 2 cups water, and ¼ cup dried lavender to a boil. Shut off the heat and steep for 20 minutes. Strain out the lavender.

18
PACIFIC RIM DISTILLING

LUKE ERRIDGE, OWNER AND DISTILLER

2-317 FORBES ROAD

UCLUELET, BC V0R 3A0

250-726-2075

ORDERS@PACIFICRIMDISTILLING.CA

PACIFICRIMDISTILLING.CA

LATITUDE 48.945145, LONGITUDE -125.565292

LUKE ERRIDGE WAS ONLY 22 WHEN HE BEGAN THE licence application process for his Pacific Rim distillery. That didn't mean he was a novice distiller—he had years of experience handed down from his grandfather's uncle, Alfie, his grandfather, and his mother. He proudly claims the title of being a fourth-generation distiller. "Uncle Alfie would distill anything," says Luke. "He would have tried to distill grass if he could have."

I met Luke at his distillery near downtown Ucluelet (pronounced *yew-kloo-let*, but the 1,600 or so villagers usually call it Ukee) and was enthusiastically greeted by Frankie, his super-friendly dog, whose ancestry includes a good percentage of coyote. She has a sweet, sympathetic dog face. Luke told me his girlfriend, Nashira Collet, and Frankie are the only ones allowed into the distilling area. Clients and tasters must

KNOWLEDGE IS IN MY HANDS NOW.
HAVE COMBINED FOUR GENERATIONS
SHIP WITH THE HIGHEST QUALITY
BRITISH COLUMBIA HAS TO OFFER
METHING TRULY SPECIAL.

Luke Erridge with his only employee, his dog, Frankie.

stay behind the live-edge wooden tasting bar, and a stack of liquor-filled boxes prevents views of the still and fermentation tanks. He did allow me a sneak peek a bit later.

Luke is an exuberant, roly-poly fellow, homespun, wearing a navy blue knitted toque in the unheated distillery. He picks up his 50-pound dog as if she were a chihuahua. He sports tattoos on his arms; body art seems to be a requirement for many distillers. He's fervently dedicated to ensuring the Pacific Rim and Barkley Sound terroir finds an expression in his vodka and gin—and that drinkers of his spirits appreciate that provenance.

He didn't set out as a distiller or an aficionado of the BC far west coast. Luke grew up in Ennismore, about 500 kilometres northeast of Toronto. With a population of about 500, the village is too small for a website, a rarity these days. Luke studied forest engineering at Laurentian University, where he

also played lacrosse. His first job brought him west to True North Forestry, a small forestry company in Nakusp, BC, but after being laid off, he began pondering his future. Would forest work be stable? Was this a moribund industry?

When the idea occurred to him that distilling might be a career path, he did his "homework" by visiting a series of bars and tasting their spirits. "None of them measured up to the stuff grandpa made in the backyard," he says. "I knew I could do better. I learned in his backyard—the Harvard of distilling. "

The steps between aspiration and reality were slow. The first step was obtaining licences to distill—a process that involves getting permission from and paying fees to federal, provincial, and municipal agencies. "It was my first business experience at age 22, 23,"

Luke says. "I had no idea what I was doing. My business plan was laughable, and the bank I approached didn't give me the time of day. And Community Futures wanted 9 percent interest! Just too much."

Fortunately, he had the "family bank" to fall back on. "My grandmother Judy lent me the money," he says. "She had faith that I could do it."

THE START-UP

He rented an empty bay in a Ucluelet light-industrial complex. Its studs were visible and the floor was covered with gravel. "My distiller grandfather, Ken Robertson, came from Ontario and helped me," says Luke. "Without him I couldn't have put up the drywall and poured concrete over the entire floor area, couldn't have made the platform for the still and fermenting tuns. We did it all by hand. I scrounged for materials and put in lots of sweat equity. It took us nearly five months."

He says the distillery has a single employee: Luke (plus Frankie, he adds, grinning). But he also receives important assistance from his girlfriend, Nashira. Although she works full-time, she keeps Pacific Rim's books and paperwork and handles social media. "She's the one who keeps me on track," says Luke.

When he first opened the distillery, he bought two 200-litre, no-name stills through the Chinese website Alibaba. One of these greets clients near the front door. He nicknamed it Patricia after his other grandmother, but its capacity was too small—he couldn't distill enough spirit to keep up with demand. Running the two small stills was too time consuming.

Luke by Pacific Rim's still.

Finding a larger but affordable still was challenging. The traditional German stills were much too costly. Even regional still producers were out of range financially. So Luke went back to the distillery equipment maker in China and, with some trepidation, ordered a 400-litre still and three fermenting tuns. "Ken and I made this crude drawing of the kind of still we wanted. Amazingly, they built and shipped it."

The still works satisfactorily, but the electrical parts were completely inadequate. Luke and an electrician friend rebuilt those components. Luke says his distilling process is not automated. "See those ammeters?" He points to the electrical boxes on the wall. "I control the process with them. I control them manually. They measure the electric current in amperes. I've learned how to do this consistently after messing up early on."

I ask him why he isn't using all his stills. "When running them at the same time, they ate right through the yeast I had available," Luke answers. "So I stuck with the 400-litre still. But I plan to put one of the 200-litre stills back in production soon."

Pacific Rim Distilling opened formally in 2017, but Luke had been distilling during the previous months, testing recipes, analyzing wild yeast, and building up stock. In the first year of operations, he'd distill a batch of vodka and bottle it on Thursday; it would run out by Saturday night. He'd then start the next batch, sometimes sleeping in the shop to monitor nighttime runs through the still. He's still amazed at the sales during that year. "The only advertising was a couple of sandwich boards," he recalls with a grin. "The local support was way more than I had anticipated."

The second year, he increased production and expanded his private liquor store accounts. Restaurants now make up about 25 percent of his sales. About 45 percent of sales are made to locals and tourists. The third year, Pacific Rim entered a higher plane—more product, more distribution. "The first year, we broke into the green," says Luke. "Since then, our income has been rising, a bit better each year. I've started to make a living."

But not everyone is able to acquire Pacific Rim's vodka and gin. "I only sell to restaurants and bars that appreciate the products and the work I put into it," Luke says adamantly. "If it's just one more bottle on their bar shelves, I don't want them to carry my spirits."

This philosophy is spelled out on a wall next to the tasting bar. In all-capital, thick chalk letters, his customers read this message:

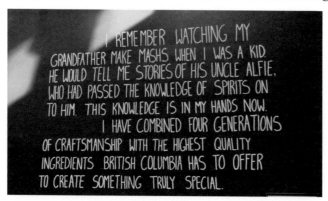

Luke's pedigree.

THE WILD YEAST

One way Luke distinguishes his vodka and gin from those of other producers is his use of wild yeast. He started hunting wild yeast years ago, but now that he has the distillery, he has chosen to ferment his spirits with wild yeast he has gathered and cultivated himself. To obtain strains of yeast, he placed a series of Mason jars with a low-sugar mash in the nearby forests. As yeast lives just about everywhere, it quickly colonized the mash.

"The contents often produce some foam as the yeast ferments," explains Luke. "After leaving the jars out for a few days, I collected them, tested the yeasts, and chose the most promising one. They're certainly not all fit for commercial use. I fished out a single cell from the most likely candidate and grew it in a petri dish with an agar medium. It worked, and I keep using that yeast. It's stored in four 55-gallon fermenters. I have to feed it continually so it makes more of itself. Think sourdough starter for bread. It's the same principle."

Does the wild yeast change the spirit leaving the still? According to Luke, the fermentation with his specific wild yeast culture, locally collected and propagated, gives his Humpback Vodka unique floral flavours. "I'm not trying to make spirits that fit into traditional categories," he says. "I'm more trying to give people an expression of Ukee and Barkley Sound."

Will Pacific Rim become a much larger distiller? Luke isn't sure, but he's committed to never sacrificing quality for volume. "This is my family's legacy," he says, "and with that comes a responsibility to respect it. I definitely want to get bigger than I am now, but if the quality is going to be affected, I won't expand. I'm already making a decent living. I am very confident that I could grow it to a much larger scale while maintaining

The places where Luke forages for wild yeast.

the quality, but it takes time. I'll never use any computerized stills. . . . Everything will always be done by hand and controlled manually. Instead of buying some automated system, I would much rather train another person and teach them the craft."

PACIFIC RIM'S PRODUCTS

Humpback Vodka is the first product out of the still. Luke says it is the result of roughly 200 years of craftsmanship passed through multiple family generations. His ancestors, he says, have passed on pre-Prohibition recipes that he has refined for modern-day palates. Humpback distinguishes itself by the use of wild yeast for its fermentation. The base input is malted barley supplied by Victoria's Phillips Brewing & Malting. Luke calls it "single malt" vodka, and he distills his vodka five times. The alcohol by volume is 40 percent.

Luke uses the vodka as the base for his Lighthouse Gin, made with nine botanicals he forages himself in the forests and fields south of the Ucluelet–Tofino junction. He flavours his gin with juniper, Nootka rose petals, salal berries, and shore pine, but he doesn't reveal the other five ingredients. "They're secret," he says. He again calls this spirit a "single malt" gin and says it's the ultimate expression of his local terroir. He distills four of his botanicals with the spirit in the pot; four other botanicals are infused through a gin basket, and salal, the ninth botanical, is steeped post-distillation. The gin has a rosy tint. The alcohol by volume is 42 percent.

Luke has distilled one barrel of single malt whisky. It's maturing in an Ontario hand-coopered cask made of Canadian white oak, with a deep "alligator skin" charred interior. Remarkably, the cask is stored on a local fishboat, and it travels the nearby ocean, sloshing its contents around and ensuring all the spirit is in continuous contact with the charred interior. Luke doesn't have to pay for this unique form of storage, but he does have to stock the fishboat with his other spirits to make sure the crew don't help themselves to the cask's contents. The whisky will not be released for several years. He plans to make more whisky when time and equipment allow.

Lighthouse Gin on its driftwood support.

Recently Luke teamed up with Zoë's Bakery & Café to produce Calm Harbour Creamer.

Zoë's is a favourite venue for Ukee locals and visitors alike. The creamer is inspired by the flavours from Zoë's classic cinnamon buns. It's blended with Pacific Rim's single malt vodka, fermented with yeast similar to the one used to rise the buns, and finished with a slight touch of orange. The creamer can flavour coffee, milk, or tea; it's not bottled and is exclusively available at Zoë's. "It's a fun project," says Luke, "in the tradition of neighbours helping neighbours."

Plans are afoot for a 2020 spirit addition: a quince liqueur. John and Gillian Edwards operate Ladysmith-based Quinceotica, a quince orchard. "John is just crazy about quince," says Luke. "We are hoping to collaborate on a unique liqueur with this uncommon fruit."

AWARDS

Despite Pacific Rim's relative youth as a company, Luke's heritage has already won him some medals. He believes that when his Humpback Vodka won a silver medal at the 2019 Canadian Artisan Spirit Competition, his grandfather, Ken, might have shed a tear.

In the same competition, his Lighthouse Gin won a bronze medal.

At the 2020 Canadian Artisan Spirit Competition, Lighthouse Gin won a silver medal, while Humpback Vodka won bronze.

The view from Ucluelet's Wild Pacific Trail, where Luke finds his wild yeasts.

FAVOURITE COCKTAILS

HUMPBACK SOUR

2 oz (60 mL) Humpback Vodka

1 oz (30 mL) simple syrup (1:1 sugar and water)

1 egg white

Juice of ½ lemon

Lemon peel

Put all the ingredients in a shaker with ice. Shake vigorously. Strain into a glass and garnish with lemon peel. Or, if you're feeling creative, substitute any kind of tea for the simple syrup.

THE HEARTWOOD

2 oz (60 mL) Lighthouse Gin

1 oz (30 mL) sweet vermouth

3–4 dashes bitters

Orange peel

Put all the ingredients in a shaker with ice. Shake vigorously. Strain into a glass and garnish with orange peel.

TOWARD
CAMPBELL
RIVER

19
ISLAND SPIRITS DISTILLERY

PETER AND VERNA KIMMERLY, OWNERS

4605 ROBURN ROAD

HORNBY ISLAND, BC V0R 1Z0

250-335-0630

ISLANDSPIRITS@OUTLOOK.COM

ISLANDSPIRITS.CA

LATITUDE 49.534391, LONGITUDE -124.653753

IT TAKES TWO FERRIES TO REACH ISLAND SPIRITS Distillery, and that is if you're starting out on Vancouver Island. But it's a worthwhile adventure—you'll get a relaxing ride across some of the Salish Sea's scenic waterways, followed by a drive across Denman and Hornby Islands, to visit Peter and Verna Kimmerly's distillery. They're located in a rural setting at the end of a long driveway.

I visited them in January, when one of the west coast's rare snowstorms had slowed ferry and road traffic to a near stand-still. Yet while crossing the islands, the community spirit was evident: where the snow piled up and only one car could pass, people would pull over and wait their turn while waving cheerfully. Island life is laid back and communal.

Peter and Verna had cleared the patch in front of the distillery, and we had ample time to discuss their history and products. Their website states, "It is our belief that the best uses of distilled spirit are to promote conversation." And conversations we had. Peter has a colourful background that didn't necessarily lead to producing spirits.

Verna was brought up in the Cowichan Valley, so life on Hornby, with its forests and farms, recalls her childhood. Peter comes from a nautical family; his father was a French Canadian naval architect, and his mother a British war bride who had been a coder for the navy. Peter is one of eight kids, and the naval family moved frequently to places such as Halifax, Ottawa, Quebec City, and Victoria. He was involved in building an 18-foot runabout from a *Popular Mechanics* blueprint when he was 11, a feat that likely determined his later career. He thought he'd be a physician, but after majoring in zoology at the University of Victoria, he found going to sea more exciting.

After serving in the Royal Canadian Navy, he jumped to the Coast Guard, where he sailed on an Arctic icebreaker, the CCGS *John A. McDonald*. He also skippered Gulf Oil's *Terry Fox*, another heavy icebreaker, from Tuktoyaktuk to Halifax. That ship was sold to the Canadian Coast Guard and is still active. After a long stint captaining ships in the Arctic for BeauDril, a Gulf Oil subsidiary, he served as a captain on BC Ferries' various routes, ending as senior master on the Hornby Island ferry route. He retired in 2009. He looks nautical, with his full but neatly trimmed white beard and captain-like bearing. Only his heavy, dark eyebrows reveal the colour hair he once had.

Verna and Peter moved from Duncan to Hornby Island in 2003 and bought a home there. Peter had a history of amateur distilling and teamed with fellow Hornby resident Dr. Naz Abdurahman, a retired organic chemistry professor, to make their first spirits. They experimented with various recipes, and their friends and neighbours were pleased to provide taste testing.

In 2009 Island Spirits submitted its products to the International Bartenders Association meeting, held in Chicago that year. Alongside that meeting, the Chicago-based Beverage Tasting Institute (Tastings.com) held a tasting event. Island Spirits won silver medals for its PHROG Premium Vodka and PHROG Gin.

"We'd wondered how the result of an icebreaker captain and chemistry professor's spirit experiments would stand up to commercial tipples," Peter recalls with glee. "We were told over and over that we should sell our spirits commercially. So we did."

Verna and Peter had bought five acres on the island, cleared some of the forest, and planted a two-and-a-half-acre orchard with apple, plum, and pear trees, as well as grapevines. "I tried to grow Jerusalem artichokes for their high sugar

Peter filling his pot still.

Peter Kimmerly by his stills.

content," says Peter. "But it would have required much more land to produce enough for our spirits."

Island Spirits got its liquor licences in 2007 and has been making its vodka, its gin, and a series of liqueurs ever since. Verna keeps order and manages the books, purchases supplies, and sometimes delivers a few cases of spirits. Naz continues to consult and performs the occasional chemical tests, while Peter ferments and distills. "Our goal is to make the best booze we're physically able to make in our retirement," says Peter.

The Kimmerlys rebuilt a workshop that once served as a truck repair place into a spacious distilling and tasting room. Some of the beams were cut from their acreage's trees. Peter also cuts his own firewood for a boiler that not only provides warmth for the distillery but also heats the couple's home a few yards away. The original experimental stills have been re- placed by two Holstein pot stills, each with a rectifying column. The first one, with a capacity of 120 litres, was built in 2011 in Eriskirch, Germany. Peter added the second, 528-litre Holstein, fabricated in Markdorf, Germany, in 2016. The latter's column is so tall that a niche had to be cut in the roof to accommodate it.

"One of our three sons is an industrial electrician," says Peter. "He installed all the wiring for our dedicated fermenting tanks and stills."

The artisan small-batch distillery uses Albertan beet sugar as its base. "Naz and I worked out the recipe," says Peter. "No starch. It's either sucrose or fructose." Along with the sugar, Peter adds yeast, molasses, vitamins B1 and B2, magnesium sulphate, and a batch of other, secret ingredients to the wash. "Our 10 fermenting vats are separated from the stills by a wall. I keep the narrow area housing the fermenting tanks at 81°F [27°C]," says Peter. "It makes the fermentation go like crazy. I get 250 litres of wash in 12 days. It's a bit slower in the winter. The wash has about 16 to 18 percent alcohol. It's a very anemic vodka."

Peter then distills the wash in one of the Holstein stills, pro-

ducing about 6,000 litres of spirits a year. "In the early days, we shipped to Alberta," he says, "because their liquor laws made economic sense. It's too costly and too regulation bound to sell to BC government liquor stores. We sell almost all our products on-site at our distillery. We have a religious following as far away as California. We deliver to yachts who sail to Hornby. Certain neighbourhoods get together and make up a large order."

Distilleries require much plumbing.

The original brand name for the vodka and gin was PHROG, a takeoff on the ubiquitous frogs that regularly serenade the Kimmerlys, and the word's beginning *pH* reflecting the scientific nature of the product. Peter and Naz say they've discovered what causes hangovers. "It's trace amounts of propanol, isopentanol, methyl butanol, and isobutanol," they state at the website. "We also learned how to get rid of them." Thus they recommend their own spirits over any other, although not in unlimited amounts.

Island Spirits, like other artisan and craft distilleries, uses a variety of botanicals to flavour its gin. But in recognition of the medieval alchemists who appreciated the medicinal value of alcohol, they have not only identified the botanicals they use to infuse their gin, but also described the healthful essence of each of these 14 botanicals on their website.

After perusing the list (reproduced here, with Island Spirits' permission), I wonder if we should start drinking gin for our health:

1. Juniper berries: Traditional to gin, the alpha pinene compound provides the spirit's astringency. It assists digestion, settles the stomach and reduces gas. Its diuretic properties have been rumoured to reduce fluid retention around sore joints. (Juniper must be included in gin to be called gin.)

2. Coriander seeds: This is the next most popular botanical used in gin. It is rumoured to ease arthritis symptoms with its anti-inflammatory properties. It also lowers LDL cholesterol.

3. Licorice root: This is common in cough syrup. It soothes bronchial and sore throat issues.

4. Cinnamon: This spice inhibits bacterial growth and is

an effective food preservative. It is often prescribed by naturopaths to reduce yeast infections. It also has been used to control blood sugars.

5. Lemon peel zest: A good source of vitamin C which helps colds have a more difficult time to get established. It also tastes good.

6. Lime peel zest: The same medicinal properties as lemon peel zest.

7. Cardamom seeds: We are getting down to trace elements here. This is also called grains of paradise. It detoxifies the body, reduces bad breath and improves circulation to the lungs.

8. Cumin seeds: This is the main ingredient in curry. It aids digestion by stimulating pancreatic enzymes and has been shown to be able to control growth of tumours.

Peter and Verna Kimmerly looking at a drawer containing botanicals.

9. Cloves: This is a powerful antioxidant. Oil of cloves is used by dentists to relieve gum pain during oral surgery.
10. Fennel seeds: Fennel has been proven to protect the liver from some toxic chemical injuries.
11. Caraway seeds: These have a soothing effect on the gastro-intestinal system.
12. Star anise: This herb has been shown to cure colic in babies. It also eases some flu symptoms.
13. Angelica root: This herb claims to reduce high blood pressure and relieve menstrual cramps.
14. Lemon grass: Citronella is made from lemon grass. It has a calming effect and is a powerful detoxifier of the liver and digestive system.

ISLAND SPIRITS' PRODUCTS

PHROG Vodka is Island Spirits' prime spirit, which, besides standing on its own, also forms the base of its gin and liqueurs. It's the first product that leaves the spirit still and allows for the many adaptations listed below. Alcohol by volume is 40 percent.

Brown Vodka is made with beer and burnt white sugar. Once combined with the firm's vodka, it tastes like single malt Scotch. Alcohol by volume is 40 percent.

PHROG Gin is infused with the 14 botanicals listed above. The gin is allowed to age and mellow to bring out its full flavour. Alcohol by volume is 43.5 percent.

Black Jelly Bean Szechuan is a liquor that tastes just as it sounds—dark licorice flavour with a jolt of spice as it clears your palate on its way to your stomach. Peter says this spirit can do double duty as a dipping sauce for oysters. Alcohol by volume is 30 percent.

Pear Brandy includes the infusion of fresh fermented pears from the Kimmerly orchard and dried pears from the Okanagan, which are then distilled and form this brandy reminiscent of Poire Williams. Alcohol by volume is 40 percent.

Aquavit is Island Spirit's vodka reborn by the addition of star anise, fennel, cumin, caraway seed, and dill. Alcohol by volume is 40 percent.

Holunderblüten is made with the colloidal suspension of elderflower tea and flavoured with glucose and lemon. Many imbibers mix this liqueur with sparkling wine. It's one of Island Spirits' most popular liqueurs. Alcohol by volume is 25 percent.

To make 75–80 bottles of Raspberry Liqueur, it takes more than 80 kilograms of raspberries. The fruit arrives in frozen blocks from an Abbotsford farm. The fruit is then infused into vodka and redistilled. Alcohol by volume is 40 percent.

Island Spirits uses ground-up, thin-skinned, whole satsuma oranges from California to produce its Orange Liqueur. Alcohol by volume is 40 percent.

The distillery also produces other small batches of vodkas enhanced by flavours including toffee and salted caramel, root beer, blackberry, green apple, hazelnut, vanilla, lemon balm, and chocolate mint. Alcohol by volume is 40 percent for all these flavoured vodkas.

Peter is considering using schisandra, a berry used in traditional Chinese medicine, to flavour a batch of vodka. Said to contain both sweet and sour flavours, the berry is included in many traditional Chinese herbal formulas for improving energy and mental health.

AWARDS

"We have a drawer full of awards," says Peter. "But we are no longer sending in samples to be judged. It's expensive and requires much paperwork. It's become boring and just not worth it. We cannot keep up with the demand for our products, not even on Hornby. So why bother?"

TOURS AND EVENTS

Besides visitors looking for their favourite spirits, families with children come to enjoy the chickens, the ducks, and the koi in the pond. And a very friendly little black and white dog greets every arriving car.

FAVOURITE RECIPE

It's simple: two-thirds gin, one-third water. On a hot day: gin plus 3 or 4 ice cubes.

20
WAYWARD
DISTILLERY

DAVE BRIMACOMBE, OWNER AND DISTILLER

2931 MORAY AVENUE

COURTENAY, BC V9N 7S7

250-871-0424

INFO@WAYWARDDISTILLERY.COM

WAYWARDDISTILLERY.COM

LATITUDE 49.669160, LONGITUDE -124.984410

MANY CRAFT DISTILLERIES ARE FAMILY BUSINESSES.
They include husband-and-wife teams, multigenerational outfits, a grandmother funding a grandson, or a daughter expanding her dad's brewery with a still. Wayward Distillery is a family of a different kind: owner Dave Brimacombe served in the Royal Canadian Air Force for a decade and a half and has drawn investors and staff from his military past, creating a tight-knit group.

During his military service, Dave travelled Canada province by province and experimented making different alcoholic beverages along the way. "I'm an alcohol tourist," he says, grinning. "A tinkerer. As I have a good palate, eventually I get a good product." He had fun fermenting hard cider, mead, and beer, which in due course led to his learning to distill. He had a small still at home for making vodka and gin. "I was producing pretty good spirits," he recalls. "Their quality gave me confidence. The science of distilling has been known for hundreds of years, so there's a lot of information available."

While still in the military, Dave began reflecting on his future. He and his ex-wife, Andrea, were drawn to distilling. But Dave, a tall, sturdy guy who sports a trimmed red beard, wondered if he should risk leaving a steady career for the uncertainties of entrepreneurship. Would it be foolish to leave the military before his full pension kicked in? Before deciding, he visited wineries, breweries, and distilleries. He also explored distilleries in Scotland.

In 2013, when the BC government gave permission for craft distilleries to establish themselves, with a tax break for the production of the first 50,000 litres, Dave knew his time had come. He explored how receptive the municipalities of Comox, Cumberland, and Courtenay would be. "Courtenay was the most interested," Dave recalls. "I would be able to open fairly quickly."

Wayward Distillery's honeybee sculpture.

So he took the risk and leased a 4,000-square-foot building in a light-industrial area of Courtenay. The free-standing structure had been home to a welding and heavy equipment shop and came with fireproof and waterproof walls, a key advantage for starting a distillery. Wayward opened in 2014, making it one of the first true craft distilleries in BC to start making spirits.

To make sure he knew the details of distilling more substantial quantities of spirits, and the business acumen it would take, Dave took a course with the American Distilling Institute that took place in Gig Harbor, Washington, and another at Dry Fly Distilling's school in Spokane. "After the workshops, I went home, felt ready to launch a distillery, started thinking about packaging, and bought a forklift," Dave says.

Funding came from his and Andrea's savings, family, maxing out credit cards, and military friends who invested, including Sara Unrau, a shareholder who is now Wayward's administrator.

Dave also chose honey as the base ingredient for his spirits—the first distillery to do so in Canada. "It was scary to use honey," he says. "No one else was doing it." But he persisted and created the company slogan "Fundamentally against the grain." Dave also asserts that Wayward is made up of a "group of unruly people fighting the evils of poor-quality spirits one bottle at a time."

Honey is up to 10 times more expensive than grain, takes more time to ferment, and can be finicky. It takes a bit more than one kilogram of honey to produce one 750-millilitre bottle of spirit.

The distillery works closely with its honey supplier, Golden Clover Apiary, located near Dawson Creek, BC. The two enterprises have flourished together: when they first started collaborating, the apiary had 300 hives. Today, it has 1,100 hives, of which Wayward sponsors 800. The honey is sent to Wayward in stainless steel 200-litre barrels.

Golden Clover also leases its bees to farms in the Fraser Valley to promote pollination. Dave says that his spirits add to food production. "First," he says, "there are more hives and bees because we base our spirits on honey. To obtain the roughly two and a half pounds of honey for one bottle of spirits requires a bee to visit about 300,000 flowers and blossoms. All these are pollinated by the bees and thus produce more flowers or apples, pears, plums, and so on. In that roundabout way, our spirits are net food producers." (A great excuse to imbibe Wayward's spirits!)

Dave has placed a couple of demonstration hives at the distillery's property to help "educate guests and the community about the value and need for healthy honeybee populations."

Wayward processes about 850 kilograms of honey a week, with a fermentation period of some two weeks. This may vary somewhat, because, Dave says, "honey has its own personality." The wash leaving the fermenting tanks is mead, which is then distilled into high-quality ethanol. He has chosen to use one type of fermentation yeast for consistency, but only after working with a zymologist to test a variety of yeasts (a zymologist is a scientist who studies the biochemical process of fermentation and its practical uses).

For the stills, Dave chose Cage and Sons Distilling Systems, initially located in Duncan but now fabricating in Lethbridge, Alberta. The same engineer designed the 200-litre still and the later Cage 1,200-litre still that run six days a week. Wayward also owns a 50-litre Holstein still found by a local fellow at an auction. "It needed some refurbishment but we were able to hook it up for experiments," says Dave. "As the honey base is expensive, we want to conduct our flavour and taste tests in a small still."

The distillery houses three 3,000-litre fermenting tanks. They were also manufactured by Cage and Sons, and their dimpled jackets are insulated so fermentation is steady.

Dave Brimacombe in his distillery.

A small pump that stirs the fermenting honey is "like a hard-working employee," Dave says.

Wayward's products are sold at farmers' markets and on-site, representing about 60 percent of sales. Liquor stores sell about 30 percent, while restaurants/bars account for the final 10 percent. It took perseverance to market the spirits to the 400 or so private liquor stores. "I took to the road on Vancouver Island and the BC interior, did one-on-one sales pitches to store owners, and led in-store taste testing," Dave says, showing me the wheeled bottle bag that contained his samples. "I also told bars and restaurants about our unique honey base that gives our vodka and gin depth. 'You want to taste this,' I'd say to everyone.

"Although honey is more expensive, and we make less profit, we've continued to outsell our projections," Dave continues. "We reached our four-year goal in two. We're making about 20,000 litres a year. We're profitable. I'm happy, but I do want to keep growing."

Wayward's distiller, Laura Carbonell.

Wayward employs the first female distiller I met on Vancouver Island, Laura Carbonell (since then I've met new distillers Kala Hadfield at Spinnakers and Shelly Heppner at Bespoke Spirits House). Laura, along with her husband, Curt, also has a military pedigree. "After leaving the military, and a few jobs, I turned left, settled in the Comox Valley, and have now worked at Wayward for five years," says Laura. "I started in fermenting and learned distilling along the way. Middle Mountain Mead taught me how to make mead."

Laura sends Wayward's best-selling product to her mum in Calgary. "Krupnik contains toasted honey," she explains. "We blend honey with water and then simmer the concoction on propane burners for many hours until it's toasted. A Polish visitor gave us her recipe, and we then checked out many more recipes on the internet. We tried a bunch of these and then styled our own version with spices and citrus. It started as a holiday drink, but demand has moved us to prepare it year-around."

She explains why many of the distillery's bins and barrels have name labels on them. "The taxman requires us to account for every bit of honey and fermented beverage we make. To track the products in different vats, we named them. The big fermentation tank is Arnold, after the Belgian patron saint of brewing," she says, referring to Arnold of Oudenburg (1040–87), a Roman Catholic saint and patron of hop pickers and Belgian brewers. "We have such names as Wee Man and Big Country, Batman and Xena. We fight over naming the receptacles."

Sam Larente is Wayward's bartender/bar manager. He's created a series of cocktail recipes. "Having a job here is a cool opportunity," he says. "I like creating the guest experience. I don't think people just want to drink. They want an experience. I call myself a 'spirit guide.' I explain the distilling process

Tipplers at the Wayward tasting bar.

and its mystique. It's still romantic to me." He notes that people today pay attention to details, to the ingredients and where they come from. "They want transparency. And west coast people support local fare." When not at the tasting bar, Sam helps with production, bottling, packaging, and labelling. Along the way, he's picking up pointers on the distilling process.

"Distilling has been around for centuries, but I believe we have a unique approach to traditional ways of creating spirits," says Dave. "Not only the honey as the base. The big producers brand everything and try to create mysteries around their alcohol. By showing how we distill through our tours and tastings, I want to demystify the distilling process. Make the process visible. Let people see how honestly it's made."

WAYWARD'S PRODUCTS

Why is it Unruly Vodka? Dave says the name harks back to the ferocious Vikings, who drank their mead from cattle horns, and to the unruliness of bees. It's based on 100 percent BC honey and is the first finished product that comes out of Wayward's stills. It's the base for all other Wayward spirits. Alcohol by volume is 40 percent.

Wayward's vodka.
Photo: Marc Phillips.

Unruly Gin starts with Wayward's vodka, and six botanicals are infused into this spirit. Originally, Wayward experimented with many more botanicals, some of them "off the wall," Dave says. "But unlike traditional juniper-heavy London dry gins, Unruly Gin is a refreshingly alternative Canadian-style gin. Our Unruly Gin has more personality because we force vodka steam through a silk bag." The silk bag contains juniper, coriander, orange peel, sarsaparilla root, cedar tips, and lavender. Alcohol by volume is 43 percent.

Krupnik Spiced Honey Liqueur is Wayward's best-selling spirit. It, like all the distillery's spirits, starts life as 100 percent BC honey. The resulting vodka is then gently flavoured with a blend of toasted honey, cinnamon, nutmeg, raw vanilla, and citrus peel. Alcohol by volume is 40 percent.

Rum traditionally derives from a sugar cane by-product, usually molasses. But Wayward doesn't import sugar from other jurisdictions. It uses its BC honey base and caramelizes it to make Drunken Hive Rum. No sugar cane derivatives in sight. Wayward ages this spirit in full-sized casks that previously held bourbon for at least 15 months. During the maturing period in

Wayward Distillery Krupnik

Krupnik is a traditional Polish sweet liqueur of grain spirit and honey. I tried this for the first time last year and fell in love. It's warm, it's spiced, and it goes just as well over ice as it does blended into a cocktail. Don't want to bring yet another bottle of wine as a hostess gift? Bring one of these instead.

WAYWARDDISTILLERY.COM
293I MORAY AVE. COURTENAY

Wayward's best-selling spirit.

the cask, the flavours from the bourbon and the charred-wood interior penetrate the spirit and create a rich and flavourful rum. The alcohol by volume is 42.5 percent.

Depth Charge Espresso and Cacao Bean Vodka Infusion has evolved from a collaboration between a small local coffee roastery, Royston Roasting Company, and Wayward's Unruly Vodka. It's a custom blend of organic fair-trade espresso and raw organic cacao nibs with Unruly Vodka. It's a great addition to coffee, or the main ingredient for a dry White Russian. As Wayward's website says, "Depth Charge is guaranteed to #MakeCoffeeGreatAgain." The alcohol by volume is 33 percent.

Cocktail Elixir 151 might cause a really "under the table" experience, so you should only wet your lips with this vodka with a 75.5 percent alcohol content. According to Dave, it was the first premium high-proof vodka available in Canada. With its high alcohol content, bartenders and individuals can create a wide variety of cocktails. The Elixir also offers a palette for making personalized infused spirits and liqueurs.

Gins aren't usually matured in barrels. But Char #3 Bourbon Barrel Aged Gin does just that. Some of Wayward's Unruly Gin finds its way into a charred barrel that previously stored bourbon. The gin leaches new flavours from the barrel over a six-month maturing period. "It's an unexpected gin for the unrepentant bourbon lover," the website notes. The alcohol by volume is 45 percent.

During the COVID-19 pandemic, Wayward began making hand sanitizer. The name on the label: W.H.O. Recommended Handrub Formulation for Distantly Social Times.

AWARDS

Wayward earned a number of medals at the 2018 Canadian Artisan Spirit Competition: gold for Unruly Vodka, Krupnik, and Depth Charge (best in class), and silver for Unruly Gin and Drunken Hive Rum. A year later, Drunken Hive Rum advanced by winning gold with distinction, while Cocktail Elixir 151 and Char #3 took silver.

TOURS AND EVENTS

Wayward gives tours of the distillery and offers samples at its tasting bar. It's also featured on culinary tours, including the Vancouver Island Spirit Path and Island Joy Rides, which organizes boutique bicycle tours that explore locally sourced food and drink. TripAdvisor recommends the distillery for a spirit-tasting experience.

FAVOURITE COCKTAILS

BLUEBERRY LEMON DROP

¾ oz (22 mL) honey syrup (1:1 honey and hot water)

¾ oz (22 mL) fresh lemon juice

½ oz (15 mL) Blueberry Lemon Shrub

½ oz (15 mL) Unruly Vodka

½ dash Suius Cherry Bitters

½ dash Clingstone Peach Bitters

3 oz (90 mL) soda water

Lemon peel

Shake the first six ingredients with ice and strain into a glass over ice. Top with the soda water, express lemon peel over the glass, and garnish.

ROSEMARY G AND T

5 oz (150 mL) soda

1 oz (30 mL) Rootside Dry Tonic Syrup

½ oz (15 mL) Unruly Gin

Lime wheel

Spanked sprig of rosemary

Build in a glass over ice. Garnish with lime and rosemary.

BROOKE LYNN HYTES

(From Olivia and Tiago @BitterQueens)

1 oz (30 mL) Drunken Hive Rum

¾ oz (22 mL) honey syrup (1:1 honey and hot water)

¾ oz (22 mL) fresh lemon juice

½ oz (15 mL) Odd Society Bittersweet Vermouth

½ oz (15 mL) Rigour & Whimsy 2016 Skin Contact Pinot Blanc

2 dashes Dillon's Orange Bitters

1 egg white

Dry shake, shake with ice, fine strain into a coupe glass, and garnish with saffron threads.

21
SHELTER POINT
DISTILLERY

PATRICK EVANS, OWNER

4650 REGENT ROAD

CAMPBELL RIVER, BC V9H 1E3

778-420-2200

INFO@SHELTERPOINT.CA

SHELTERPOINT.CA

LATITUDE 49.876941, LONGITUDE -125.126487

PATRICK EVANS GREW UP ON A DAIRY FARM 20 minutes from where his distillery is today. His family has farmed here for more than a century. When he was a youth, he, his dad, and his two brothers made sure the 300 cows were milked every day and that all the farm equipment remained operational and clean. "When you run a dairy farm, you're a generalist and a mechanic," says Patrick. "You're always building, always repairing, always making things."

I met Patrick after crunching through more than a foot of snow in January—an unusual event for the east coast of Vancouver Island. He's a great storyteller, self-deprecating, exuberant, with a good sense of humour. Clad in a double layer of plaid shirts, he told me his philosophy of enhancing Vancouver Island's agriculture, about being part of and working with a multigenerational family, and how much he revered his father, Norman Evans, a former dairy farmer who never quit working and was intimately involved in the distillery's early days.

I sniffed the piquant aroma of fermenting barley as we sat in deep leather chairs that almost swallowed me, near a couple of fireplaces in a room that flanks the area housing the three stills. The room is separated from the distilling portion by a wall containing nine etched-glass windows by local artist Robert Lundquist. Each window depicts an aspect of traditional spirit making. The room hosts the meetings, receptions,

Patrick Evans.

Aerial view of Shelter Point.
Courtesy Shelter Point Distillery.

and weddings that take place at Shelter Point during warmer seasons.

Patrick's father was a practical as well as an inspirational man. "One of my dad's favourite sayings was, 'To be successful, just work a half a day every day. It doesn't matter if it's the first 12 hours or the second 12.' He also declared that you can be useful or useless. It's your choice."

The practicality manifested itself when one day Norman Evans said, "We have to do some succession planning. And we should figure it out now—figure out how we should divide the dairy farm." Decisions were made, and with his portion, Patrick and his family bought 380 acres on the Strait of Georgia from the University of British Columbia (UBC), which had used the property as an agricultural research farm.

The acreage is in the Agricultural Land Reserve, so it can be used only for agricultural purposes. It has forests, salmon-bearing streams, wetlands, fields, eagles, deer, and bears. The Oyster River delineates the property's southern border. With a 2,000-metre oceanfront, Shelter Point is one of Canada's few remaining oceanfront farms. The land is also associated with a happy coincidence for Patrick. In 1962, the New York stockbroker Barrett Montford bequeathed this land and another nearby property to UBC with the stipulation that it should be farmed for 20 years. "What I find so gratifying is that Montford bought a portion of the acreage I now farm from my grandfather in 1948," says Patrick. "I'm firmly rooted here."

When Patrick first brought the farm back into the family in 2006, he was unsure what type of farming specialty he might pursue. "We had 250 heifers in the beginning," he recalls. "They were raised for beef. A year later we'd sold our cranberry farm, and by this time, my dad, James Marinus, and I decided to start a distillery." James Marinus has worked with Patrick for more than 30 years and is Shelter Point's master distiller.

"I never let fear and good judgment get in the way," Patrick quips.

In 2007, as part of grounding themselves in whisky making, they toured Scotland and explored many "lovely little pubs." Although they certainly didn't visit all of the more than 100 Scotch distilleries, Patrick was captured by the idea that whisky must be made from barley distilled in a copper pot still and then matured in oak casks for at least three years. He has the land to grow barley and enough barns and sheds to store thousands of whisky-filled barrels.

He also learned that Scotland had exported £2.5 billion worth of Scotch the previous year. (In 2018, the latest data available, Scotland exported £4.7 billion, or about C$8 billion, worth of Scotch.) "I said to myself, 'I'd like a fraction of that,'" Patrick says with a grin. "After we came home, my wife and four daughters decided that cows weren't very glamorous."

Patrick believes strongly in "value-added agriculture in British Columbia and Vancouver Island." He notes there's been a huge decline in dairy farming. "While maybe 30 years ago we had 130 dairy farms on Vancouver Island, today we have about 40. I thought that making whisky would be a higher value-added agricultural product. I want to sow, grow, and reap the grain myself and distill it into great products. I want the whole process, from field to flask, and then export our local bounty around the world. Until recently, we've had nothing like that on the Island. I see it as our own little renaissance in agriculture. It's agricultural diversification. The process gives me tons of micro moments of joy."

STARTING THE DISTILLERY

James Marinus designed the distillery building with its copper-clad roof. It took three years to build and opened in 2010. It's purpose built and has turned into a magnificent, elegant structure, with a soaring wood ceiling milled from trees on the property. "We'd raised barns in the past," says Patrick. "That gave us the confidence to construct as much of the distillery as we could." A shelf about two-thirds up the wall, above the stonework on the lower portion, carries outdated barrels wired to beam light onto the ceiling and the hefty supports, highlighting the mellow wood. The building imparts a lovely, warm feeling. "All the materials are better than required by the building code," Patrick says proudly.

Two massive Forsyths pot stills—built in Scotland—are supported by a raised wooden platform, allowing for plumbing, controls, and easy access from below. A spirit safe is positioned between the burnished copper stills. Along the wall, a series of stainless steel fermentation tanks fabricated by Newlands Systems in Prince Edward Island emit their bubbling carbon dioxide. A third still, a column still manufactured by Victoria-based Specific Mechanical Systems, flanks the pot stills and distills the vodka and gin. A good part of these two products is shipped to China and Japan. "It's easier and less expensive to ship to Asia than to distribute to BC's private liquor stores," Patrick remarks.

The company distills two shifts daily, and James, the head distiller, was sleeping after his night shift. But he'd told me during my first visit to Shelter Point that the team is continually experimenting. "We have no history like the Scots," he said. "And we lack their strict rules and traditions of Scotch distilling.

Shelter Point's whisky storage. Photo: Marc Phillips.

So we have the freedom to experiment with different grains, like rye, oats, and wheat. To blend different grains. To ask, 'Do we sell now or wait?' Although we do have to balance time as there's an expense to waiting—it certainly adds to overhead costs."

Shelter Point is now the largest artisan spirit producer on Vancouver Island. Patrick uses his multitude of former farm buildings and sheds to store more than 2,500 whisky-filled barrels, with more spirits added weekly. The age of the whisky ranges from last week to 10.5 years.

About 80 percent of the spirit-making barley is grown on Shelter Point's own land. Until recently, part of the property was devoted to raising raspberries, a good cash-flow crop that was sold to Smucker's jams in Washington State. The berries have now been phased out. "I want to grow more barley so I can be more self-sufficient," says Patrick. "Right now, we grow barley on 250 acres, producing 500 tonnes of grain in a good weather year." The barley grown on-site is sent to be malted at Gambrinus Malting in Armstrong, BC. After the now-germinated barley returns, Shelter Point uses 5,000 kilograms of grain a day.

Shelter Point's primary focus is on making whisky, although the distillery produces vodka and gin too. For the first few years, the distillery sold a series of flavoured vodkas; these have been discontinued. "Everyone's in the vodka business," says Patrick, "but from the beginning we decided that whisky was the best value-added agricultural product, so we're continually ramping up production." Moreover, Shelter Point submits that its clean water, retrieved from an underground aquifer, and the

The pot stills and fermentation tanks. Photo: Marc Phillips.

"unique, temperate rainforest climate, [where] even the sunsets and sea air become integral," engender whiskies without peer.

In 2020, Shelter Point released it fourth whisky presentations. They are available at private liquor stores and are also sold in Japan, China, Norway, and Australia. "Foreign sales are not huge," says Patrick, "but they're increasing."

Also in 2020, the first release of triple-distilled Irish-style whiskeys took place.

Shelter Point continues to ramp up its whisky production and add to its maturing stock. It also focuses on foreign exports and growing its market share in North America.

A further goal is to establish the distillery's own malting plant, a move that will eliminate the shipping of farm-grown grain to Armstrong, BC, for malting.

THE DISTILLING PROCESS

When the distillery first began operating, Master Distiller Mike Nicolson spent six months on-site and introduced James Marinus to the finer points of distilling. Patrick invites distillers to visit, taste-test the new make and more mature whiskies, and discuss the distilling process. "Having the one-on-one discussions with different distillers, it's like talking with different chefs," says Patrick. "They all have different recipes."

The distilling process starts with a tonne (2,000 kilograms) of malted, milled barley poured into the mash tuns. Hot water converts the grains' starch into sugar water, or wort. The sugary water is then fermented. I peered into a couple of churning tuns; the surfaces were covered with thick mushroom-coloured layers of froth gurgling away. The resulting wash is then piped to the stills, and during the stripping run, when heat separates the alcohol from the water, the alcohol vapours travel into a cooling tube and then condense into what's called low wine, with an alcohol content of around 30 percent. It's during the second run through the still that the low wine turns into ethanol, with a purity of up to 90 percent. The distiller makes the cuts—heads, hearts, and tails. Starting with the same wash, the pot stills are used to make only the artisanal single malt whiskies, while the column still makes CanadaOne Vodka and Hand Foraged Botanical Gin.

The hot water leaving the stills is collected in hot water tanks and reused in the mashing tuns. The spent grain—the barley residue after fermentation—is composted during the summer, or spread around the property in winter. "We have lots of swans, geese, and other birds visiting our fields who like the warm, 70°C [158°F] grain leftovers we disperse," says Patrick.

The fermentation tanks.

"The mash still has micronutrients. And all those birds are our unpaid natural fertilizers."

During distillations, the pot still's copper innards extract the sulphur that yeasts leave behind. These sulphuric compounds stick to the pot's surface and prevent the spirit from tasting bitter. After about five days of distilling, the pot must be cleaned with citric acid to remove these built-up sulphuric compounds and ensure the next wash put into the still has good contact with copper.

Cleaning a large pot still can be an onerous task. Shelter Point has invented a method to make the job much easier. The team has installed a steel pipe crowned with a swivelling, perforated head in the middle of the pot. Under pressure, the head disperses the citric acid that dissolves the sulphur. Think of a dishwasher flinging water through the dishes—the citric dispenser works similarly. After a rinse with clear water, the pot is ready to distill its next batch.

After the second distillation, the clear grain alcohol is piped into casks to mature for a minimum of three years and a day. Most of these casks come from Kentucky, from such bourbon makers as Jim Beam and Jack Daniel's. "We mostly use American oak casks," says Patrick. "Their interior can be charred to number four, which is the heaviest burn, or it can be lightly toasted, number one. The casks arrive here, 288 per truckload. We often ask for newly vacated, single-use bourbon casks, as these remain moist. In the summer heat, we fill casks quickly from our ethanol-filled tanker truck before they dry out, but the winter gives us a bit more time before filling." All these casks are stored in Shelter Point's various warehouses in triple layers separated by pallets. The casks are stored vertically.

The final step of the distilling process is the tasting and testing of the whiskies as they mature. James and fellow distiller Leon Webb "are out there continually with their whisky thieves sniffing and tasting," says Patrick. "It's a constant sensory analysis. On a scale of 1 to 10, a whisky earning an 8 might be getting close to a release. If it's a 1 or 2 after some years, maybe it's time to revat it. The cask might be old and depleted. If so, we cut it in half and sell it as a planter. Furniture makers refashion the staves into new furniture."

THE DISTILLERS AND OTHER SHELTER POINTERS

James Marinus has worked with Patrick for more than three decades, first on the farm and its various enterprises, then in the distillery. Over the years, he has served as Shelter Point's architect when designing the distillery building, become head distiller, and been intimately involved in every aspect of spirit

James Marinus.
Photo: Marc Phillips.

production. But besides distilling and planning innovative whiskies, he can also plow, handle a screwdriver, and pitch in wherever needed.

The Scotland-born distiller Leon Webb joined Shelter Point four years ago. He first studied economics at Heriot-Watt University in Edinburgh and then earned his master's in international banking. He had a good banking job but didn't find staring at numbers on a screen very rewarding. Having grown up in the Spey River region near the Highlands, an area known for its many distilleries, he figured distilling was in the blood. "Although," he says, "I only had my first taste of whisky, a proper Scotch, at age 20."

Making a radical decision, he spurned banking and enrolled again at Heriot-Watt, this time to earn his master of science in brewing and distilling. His thesis focused on creating a new gin that incorporated hand-harvested macro kelp, creating sweet and salty, umami flavours. He also met Canadian Lydia Fisher at an Edinburgh student pub, an event that brought about another major change in his life.

His first spirit-related job was at the Isle of Harris Distillery in the Outer Hebrides. It's located in a small village with 2,000 inhabitants. Marriage brought the couple to Victoria, where, after some consulting, Leon joined Victoria Distillers as master distiller. "It was a new challenge in a new world," he says.

At Victoria Distillers, with Dave Clark and Peter Hunt, he developed Empress 1908 Gin with its indigo colour (see chapter 7).

"It has drinkability, good bar appeal, flair, and uniqueness," he explains. But despite the "blue gin" success, he realized his heart longed for whisky. When Patrick needed a second distiller, Leon and he agreed to work together for four months to assess their compatibility. It worked wonderfully. "I really like the grain-to-glass concept,'" Leon says. "It's great being involved from planting to harvesting, driving a tractor. Everyone pitches in. We're farm based, we grow the barley here, use good water from our own aquifer, and breathe good Salish Sea air. Patrick allows us to innovate and experiment with different casks and blendings. I want our whiskies to be local, to reflect British Columbia.

Distiller Leon Webb.

My wife, Lydia, now does the marketing and social media for Shelter Point. And I'm 30 minutes away from snowboarding on Mount Washington!"

Patrick's son-in-law, Jacob Wiebe, married to Patrick's daughter Emily, keeps the books and manages the daily business affairs. He first came to the distillery as a carpenter for a roof repair. "Romance bloomed. He never left," says Patrick. "He handles our paperwork for the government, and such things as the raspberry sales and its transborder regulations. Besides ordering bourbon casks from Kentucky, he's developed a nose for finding casks that may give new flavour profiles to Shelter Point's whiskies, including Quails' Gate red wine barrels, Laphroaig casks, sherry butts, and blackberry wine casks." Jacob serves as Shelter Point's "ambassador" and teaches master classes on spirit making across Canada, in Seattle, and in New York. He and Leon taught a master class on Vancouver Island–made whisky at the 2020 Canadian Whisky Awards, an event that attracts whisky makers and aficionados from around the world.

In addition, two of Patrick's daughters, Tatum and Cicily, work in the bottling facility. During the summer, they welcome visitors and manage the tasting bar.

SHELTER POINT'S PRODUCTS

The barley fields in Patrick's acreage can differ markedly. If a field has stony soil, the kernels will be small, while rich soil will produce plump kernels. Parcels of land are so different that some of the harvest is kept separate. The resulting whisky is named after the field—for example, the Montford field produces its own Montford District Lot 141 Single Grain Whisky. It uses unmalted barley.

These are the facts for Shelter Point's single malt whiskies:

- They are distilled in the Forsyths pot stills.
- They are produced in small batches and distilled twice.
- The whiskies' colours are natural and non-chill filtered.
- Their bottle size is 750 millilitres, with Vinolok glass closures.
- Their alcohol by volume isn't skimpy: it ranges from 46 to 59.7 percent.

All spirit makers tout their own products. One way to judge the quality of a whisky is to consult *Jim Murray's Whisky Bible 2020*. Murray, who's known around the world for the whisky rankings in his *Bible*, scores Shelter Point's whiskies in the 90s. What does that mean? Out of 100 as the top score, 90–93.5 is "brilliant"; 94–97.5 is the score for "superstar whiskies that give us a reason to live." Below, I've included Murray's score for each whisky he has judged.

Artisanal Single Malt Whisky is Shelter Point's most prolific whisky and uses the farm's malted, two-row barley as a base. It matures in American oak casks that previously stored bourbon. Its alcohol by volume is 45 percent. *Jim Murray's Whisky Bible 2020* score: 94.5.

Smoke Point Whisky starts as single-malt whisky and un-malted barley whisky and is aged for five years in American oak, ex-bourbon casks. The spirit is then transferred and finished for eight months in casks previously used by Islay-based Laphroaig's peated whisky. This limited edition consists of only 1,044 hand-numbered bottles. The whisky picks up the flavours of the American oak cask bourbon and then the peated whisky from the ex-Islay casks, making it a sweet, smoky, and complex tipple. New batches are maturing and will be released after at least five years in their casks. Its alcohol by volume is 55 percent.

To create its limited-edition Artisanal Cask Strength Whisky, uncut and straight from the cask, Shelter Point select-ed two barrels of triple-distilled unmalted Shelter Point barley whisky and combined them with two casks of rye, creating a rich, multilayered, and spicy spirit. Its alcohol by volume is 58.4 percent. *Jim Murray's Whisky Bible 2020* score: 91.

French Oak Double Barreled Whisky, Shelter Point's fourth double-barrelled whisky, results from a special collaboration with BC's prominent Quails' Gate Winery. The distillers hand selected malted and unmalted whisky in American oak casks where they'd matured for four years and then finished them for another 152 days in French oak wine barrels previously home to Quails' Gate Foch Reserve. Its alcohol by volume is 50 percent. *Jim Murray's Whisky Bible 2020* score: 94.

Montfort District Lot 141 is a truly unique field-to-flask whisky, deriving its name from the very lot where the single-grain barley was grown. The whisky has matured on-site in either American oak or French oak casks. "It's a proud product of our distillery home," Shelter Point's website states. Only 1,224 bottles were made in this limited edition. Its alcohol by volume is 50 percent. *Jim Murray's Whisky Bible 2020* score: 92.

Single Cask Rye is Shelter Point's first single cask, available only at the distillery and online. Only 206 hand-numbered bottles have been filled. The whisky is made from 100 percent rye and picks up influences of bourbon from the American oak cask. Its alcohol by volume is 59.7 percent.

CanadaOne Vodka.

CanadaOne Vodka, made in small batches, is triple-distilled and filtered through activated charcoal. CanadaOne is a popular spirit not only for its pure, smooth taste but also for its cheerful maple-leaf-decorated bottle. A good portion of this vodka is exported to Asia. Its alcohol by volume is 46 percent.

Hand Foraged Botanical Gin is first distilled through Shelter Point's copper pot still, then again through the column still with its 10 plates. The base ingredient is two-row barley grown on-site. The botanicals include juniper, coriander, cardamom, cassia, licorice root, orrisroot, angelica, orange peel, grapefruit peel, lemon peel, and cubeb (the dried unripe berries of a tropical shrub of the pepper family). These spices are macerated for 24 hours. The gin starts with column-distilled neutral spirit, which is then redistilled with its botanicals. The alcohol by volume is 59.7 percent.

Shelter Point also makes a liqueur. One day, Patrick's daughter Megan said to her dad, "I don't like vodka, Dad. Can't you give me a nectar, something smooth and sweet? It rains here all winter, and we need some sunshine." Patrick challenged Megan to develop such a drink. The result? The aptly named Sunshine Liqueur is safeguarded in a barrel-shaped bottle. Megan uses her dad's quadruple-distilled, charcoal-filtered, neutral-grain spirits as its base, laces it with what-could-be-more-Canadian-than-maple-syrup, and adds natural orange flavouring and chai spice. It's called Orange Spice Maple and evokes the golden colours of these ingredients. The alcohol by volume is 30 percent, and it's delish! Well done, Megan.

In the first quarter of 2020, Shelter Point shut down its liquor production and switched to manufacturing medical-grade hand sanitizer to support the fight against the COVID-19 pandemic. This is what the company wrote about their decision: "Our distillers will be working double shifts over the weeks and months ahead to produce enough sanitizer to supply as many hospitals, health authorities, medical centres, municipal and provincial services as possible. Our number one priority is to ensure that first responders have ample supplies in order to do their jobs and save lives."

AWARDS

Shelter Point has submitted only whiskies to competitions. As whiskies require three years to mature and Shelter Point doesn't submit new makes to contests, its awards are fairly recent.

In 2020, Smoke Point Whisky, aged in ex-Islay casks, won Best Canadian Grain and Single Cask, while Quails' Gate Old Vines Foch Reserve secured Best Canadian Single Malt—both at the prestigious World Whiskies Awards in London, England. At the January 2020 Canadian Whisky Awards in Victoria, Single Cask Rye and Smoke Point Single Grain Whisky both captured gold. During the same event, Shelter Point's whiskies took home silver medals for Artisanal Cask Strength, Artisanal Single Malt Double Barrel, Montfort District Lot 141, Single Cask Old Vines Foch Reserve, and Wine and Beyond Exclusive Single Malt.

TOURISM AND EVENTS

In 2019 more than 18,000 visitors toured the distillery. All these folks were greeted by Brian Ingle, who calls himself the distillery's "spirit advisor." He has been leading tours of the distillery, explaining the distilling process and the farm surroundings since the distillery was established. He's another great storyteller and is on hand during the tourist season, introducing people to the "field to flask" concept.

Shelter Point hosts events like fundraisers, weddings, and community activities.

FAVOURITE COCKTAILS

PEAR NECESSITIES

1½ oz (45 mL) Shelter Point Artisanal Cask Strength Whisky

¾ oz (22 mL) Tugwell Creek Solstice Mead

½ oz (15 mL) demerara syrup (1:1 demerara sugar and water)

½ oz (15 mL) fresh lemon juice

½ oz (15 mL) Xante pear liqueur

Shake and double-strain in a large coupe. Serve neat. Add a pear fan.

A NEW FASHIONED TWIST ON THE OLD FASHIONED

1 sugar cube

3 dashes Angostura Bitters

1 orange slice

2 oz (60 mL) Shelter Point Premium Whisky

In a glass tumbler, crush the sugar cube with Angostura Bitters. Add the orange slice and gently press in with a muddler to release some of the juice. Add in 3–4 ice cubes and pour over whisky. Give a stir before serving.

GLOSSARY

absinthe: A spirit (not a liqueur) flavoured with anise, wormwood, fennel, and other herbs. It's been called the "cocaine of the 19th century." It's usually green in colour and is likely to have a very high alcohol-by-volume content.

ABV: Alcohol by volume, usually expressed in percentages. For example, a bottle of gin may contain 43 percent ABV.

activated charcoal: A substance that purifies a spirit after distillation. Often used to filter vodka.

angel's share: The portion of the alcohol in a wooden barrel or cask that's lost to evaporation.

aqua vitae: Latin for "water of life." The Gaelic version associated with Scotch and Irish whiskies is *Uisge Beatha*.

barrel or cask: A wooden cylindrical container made of wooden staves—usually oak—and held together with steel hoops. They store various types of alcoholic beverages as they mature.

botanicals: Spices, fruits, and herbs used to flavour vodka, gin, liqueurs, and other alcohol-based drinks.

bourbon: Whiskey made from a mash containing at least 51 percent corn, distilled at a maximum of 160 proof, aged at no more than 125 proof for a minimum of two years in new charred oak barrels.

bung: The stopper used to seal a barrel. It fits into the bunghole.

charring: The process that sets fire to the interior of barrels, creating a layer of charred wood. Distillers can choose from four levels of char. Level one burns for 15 seconds, level two burns for 30 seconds, level three for 35 seconds, and level four for 55 seconds. Level four is called alligator char because of its bumpy appearance. Lighter chars are called toast, light toast, or medium toast.

column still: In a column still, steam rises up while the wash descends from the top through several levels of perforated plates, or coils. One of its advantages is that it can distill continually, while a pot still distills in batches.

condensation: When a vapour changes to liquid during distillation.

cuts: The separation of the distillate into heads, hearts, and tails during the spirit run.

distillation: The process that separates alcohol from water. Alcohol evaporates at a lower temperature than water and evaporates first. It is then condensed back into liquid form.

ethanol: Also called grain alcohol, ethyl alcohol, or pure alcohol, it is a clear, colourless liquid that has been distilled to a purity of 90 percent or higher.

feints: Another term for tails, mostly used in the UK.

fermentation: The process by which yeast and enzymes transform sugar into alcohol and carbon dioxide.

fermenter: A large metal vat where the mash of cooked grains, honey, cider or other base ingredients, meet the yeast. As they mingle, the yeast begins to act on sugars in the input, and fermentation occurs over a few days or weeks. This produces alcohol within the mash and turns it into wash.

foreshots: Another term for heads, mostly used in the UK.

gin: A distilled spirit made with juniper. Other flavourings are usually added as well.

heads: The first section of the wash that exits the still's spirit run. This part of the distillate is high in impurities, contains methanol, and is often used as a solvent or biofuel. Heads are sometimes called foreshots.

hearts: The drinkable part of a distillate. Heads, hearts, and tails are separated by the distiller's skills.

infusion: The soaking or submersing of spices, herbs, fruits, and seaweed before or during the distillation process. It can also be accomplished by placing a gin basket or a silk bag inside the still and passing vapours through it.

liqueur: A spirit with added sugar and flavourings.

low wine: The name of the wash after it has passed through a still during its stripping run.

maceration: The breaking of botanicals into pieces or crumbs to expose a larger surface area during infusion.

malted barley: Barley that has been germinated in water and then dried to stop germination. Malted barley (or any malted grain) contains enzymes that convert starches into fermentable sugars. Yeasts feed on these sugars in fermentation tanks. These enzymes are not present in unmalted grains; unmalted grains thus produce lower sugar content.

mash: The mix of cooked grains and water that releases the sugars from starch.

mash tub or mash tun: A large tub where grains are combined with water and cooked to soften them and break down the starch into simple sugars before the resulting wort is transferred to the fermenter. Mash tuns are usually made from stainless steel, contain a heating mechanism, and are insulated to retain heat.

mead: A beverage resulting from fermentation of honey and water. Several distilleries on Vancouver Island and the Gulf Islands use honey as the base for their spirits.

milling: Crushing the grain to make the starch or sugar more available for enzyme action during malting.

muddler: A tool bartenders use to crush ingredients for cocktails.

nose: A spirit's aroma.

oaking: Maturing a spirit in an oak cask, or with oak sticks or chips.

peating: Smoking malted barley with peat to give it a smoky flavour.

pot still: A batch distillation unit used to distill wash. To make Scotch and other whiskies usually requires a copper pot still.

proof: Measurement of an alcoholic beverage on a scale. In Canada, a 100-proof spirit contains 50 percent alcohol.

proofing: The process of lowering alcohol strength by adding water.

rum: A spirit that uses molasses as a main ingredient. In British Columbia, to qualify their rum as a craft spirit, rum makers use BC honey as the main ingredient.

saccharify: To convert to sugar. It takes place during the mashing stages and gets the wort ready for fermentation.

Scotch: A whisky made in Scotland. Whiskies distilled elsewhere may not call themselves Scotch. Scotch whisky is not a uniform spirit. According to Wikipedia, Scotch is divided into five categories: single malt whisky, single grain whisky, blended malt whisky, blended grain whisky, and blended whisky. All Scotch whisky must be aged in oak barrels for at least three years.

sparge: To spray water on a mash to get the last bit of sweetness out of the grain.

spirit run: The final distillation producing pure ethanol.

stripping run: The process of running the wash through a still without making cuts to subtract alcohol. The resulting low wine is redistilled.

tails: The last segment of ethanol after a spirit run; this spirit is high in impurities and is usually sent back to the still for redistillation with other batches of wash. Also called feints.

wash: The liquid drained from a fermenter.

whisky thief: A tubular instrument, often made of glass, that removes a sample from a barrel to test for taste and maturity.

wort: The sugary water drained from the mash.

yeast: A living organism that feeds on fermentable sugars, transforming them to beverage alcohol, congeners, carbon dioxide, and heat. In the fermentation process, yeast converts simple sugars to ethanol.

zymology: The science that studies the biochemical process of fermentation and yeasts.

ANNOTATED RESOURCES

PRINTED SOURCES

Broom, Dave. *Gin: The Manual*. London: Mitchell Beazley, 2015. Canadian gins appear only once in this volume. The introduction, with the history of gin, is worth reading.

Broom, Dave. *Whisky: The Manual*. London: Mitchell Beazley, 2014. As British Columbia craft distilleries opened only after the BC regulations changed in 2013, only commercial whiskies are included. But Broom's introduction describing the history of whisky making is highly informative.

De Kergommeaux, Davin. *Canadian Whisky: The New Portable Expert*. Toronto: Appetite by Random House, 2017.

De Kergommeaux, Davin, and Blair Phillips. *The Definitive Guide to Canadian Distilleries: The Portable Expert to Over 200 Distilleries and the Spirits They Make (From Absinthe to Whisky, and Everything in Between)*. Toronto: Appetite by Random House, 2020. Briefly covers the many craft distilleries across Canada.

Gately, Iain. *Drink: A Cultural History of Alcohol*. New York: Gotham Books, 2008. Covers much history of the grape and grain, and how it has affected cultures mostly in the Western world. The book contains a myriad of interesting facts.

"How I Did It: Matt Phillips." *Business in Vancouver*, March 24, 2014.

Hynes, Gary. *Island Wineries of British Columbia*. Victoria: TouchWood Editions, 2013.

"Liquid Fire: The Arabs Discovered How to Distil Alcohol." *Economist*, December 18, 2003.

Marotta, Stefanie. "Trouble Brewing: Is Canada's Craft-Beer Industry Headed for a Spill?" *Globe and Mail*, January 24, 2020.

Murray, Jim. *Jim Murray's Whisky Bible 2020*. An annual guide that ranks all the nearly 20,000 whiskies produced in the world. Northamptonshire, UK: Dram Good Books, 2020.

Okrent, Daniel. *Last Call: The Rise and Fall of Prohibition*. New York: Scribner, 2011. Describes how Prohibition arose and fell in the US, and its long-term influence on the US and Canada.

Stott, John C. *Island Craft: Your Guide to the Breweries of Vancouver Island*. Victoria: TouchWood Editions, 2019.

ELECTRONIC RESOURCES

There are numerous articles about distilling, its history, liquor in general, specific alcoholic beverages, alcohol-producing companies' backgrounders, and so on, on the internet. Here are just a few.

Difford's Guide. diffordsguide.com. Provides a wealth of information on alcoholic spirits and cocktails.

Encyclopaedia Britannica Online. "Distilled Spirit." britannica .com/topic/distilled-spirit. An excellent introduction to distilled spirits, written in clear language.

Iberian Coppers. "History of Alcohol Distillation." copper -alembic.com/en/page/history-of-alcohol-distillation.

Jarvis, Brad. *Whisky 101.* The Whisky Professor. thewhiskyprofessor.com/wp-content/uploads/2012/07 /whisky101_web1.pdf. A simple but informative book in PDF format explaining how whisky is made.

Wiebe, Joe. "The History of BC Craft Beer—Part 2." BC Ale Trail, April 28, 2017. bcaletrail.ca/history-bc-craft-beer-part-2.

Wikipedia. "Liquor." en.wikipedia.org/wiki/Liquor. Describes the history of distilling, and the effects of alcohol on humans.

Wikipedia. "List of Cocktails." en.wikipedia.org/wiki/List_of _cocktails#By_mixer. Offers a long list of cocktails and their various mixes.

ACKNOWLEDGEMENTS

I thank all the owners and distillers, and their spouses, family, and staff members, who gave me their time, told me their life stories, and explained their approach to spirit entrepreneurship. I enjoyed meeting them, learning about their devotion to their craft, and discovering the myriad and serendipitous ways that led to their launching a distillery.

My appreciation goes to Dale Miller, editor of *British Columbia Magazine*, who gave me an early assignment to learn about Vancouver Island's burgeoning craft and artisan distilleries, an assignment that eventually led to this guide. I also thank Marc and Judith Phillips for accompanying me on part of the "distillery trail," and Marc for his excellent photographs.

I thank former senator Pat Carney for her encouragement and helping to ensure the concept of the book would not get lost.

The thoughtful crew at TouchWood Editions helped get this guide off the ground. Publisher Taryn Boyd and I had helpful and heartening discussions on structuring this book. Editor Kate Kennedy oversaw the step-by-step production and ensured all of us met deadlines. I thank editor Meg Yamamoto who conducted a careful and respectful edit of the manuscript, catching errors and omissions, improving the flow of words, and making the entire guide more complete and informative.

Designer Sydney Barnes used her artistic eye to choose the right fonts, position the photos in the right places, and laid out the distillery book in such a way that it will be delightful to thumb through and read. Thanks, Sydney. I also appreciate the talents of publicist Tori Elliott, who markets all of TouchWood's books with zest and dedication.

And, of course, I thank my husband, David Sanborn Scott, who patiently and cheerfully accompanied me to the various distilleries, and who always read and edited my draft chapters as they emerged from the printer.

I raise a glass to you all: shláinte, proost, santé.